# MANDALA MAGIC

## A Coloring Expedition Of Our Diverse World

## 101 Mandalas

*Kami Moon*

In a world where dreams and reality danced together, there existed a magical coloring book named "Mandala Magic." This enchanting book was no ordinary coloring book; it held the secrets of mandalas from different cultures around the world, each one a portal to an extraordinary adventure.

The moment you opened its pages, you were transported to a realm of fantasy and discovery, where mandalas from various cultures adorned each page. One mandala, inspired by the intricate Celtic knots of Ireland, invited you to fill its mesmerizing patterns with a burst of colors. As you did so, you could almost feel the ancient stones of Irish castles under your fingers, all the while staying within the soothing embrace of mandala art.

Another page, you found yourself immersed in the vibrant culture of Japan, where a stunning cherry blossom mandala awaited your artistic touch. It beckoned you to wander through sakura-lined paths, take part in traditional tea ceremonies, and gaze upon the majestic Mount Fuji. Your coloring strokes seemed to whisper the poetry of the land of the rising sun, all within the harmonious contours of the mandala.

Next, a tribal-inspired mandala transported you to the heart of Africa, where you could almost sense the rhythm of distant drums and feel the warm African sun on your skin. With every color you added, you journeyed deeper into the rich tapestry of the continent's traditions and wildlife, all while intricately connected through the mandala's design.

Further along, a Mayan-inspired mandala drew you into the mysteries of ancient Central America. As you filled its shapes with colors, you uncovered the secrets of long-lost civilizations and the wonders of lush rainforests, all woven into the mandala's intricate web.

With every turn of the page, you traversed a new culture, each one more captivating than the last, always accompanied by the harmonious symmetry of mandala art. "Mandala Magic" wasn't just a coloring book; it was a passport to explore the beauty and diversity of cultures from around the world through the intricate lines and patterns of mandalas. It became a vessel for your creativity, a source of relaxation and joy, and an invitation to discover the magic that lies within both the world's cultures and the art of mandalas. Embrace this enchanting journey and let your imagination take flight as you embark on an extraordinary coloring adventure across cultures, continents, and the mesmerizing world of mandalas.

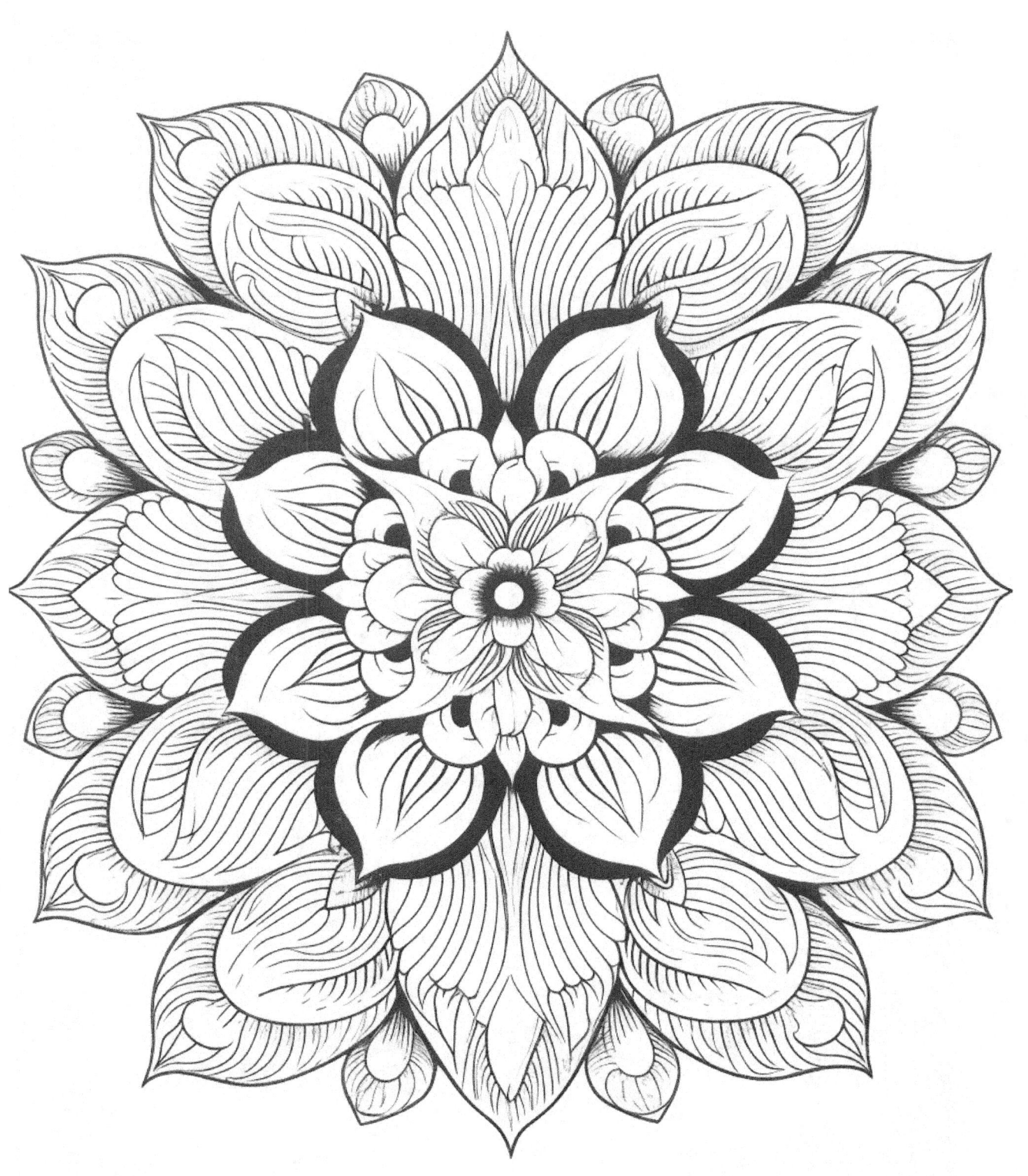

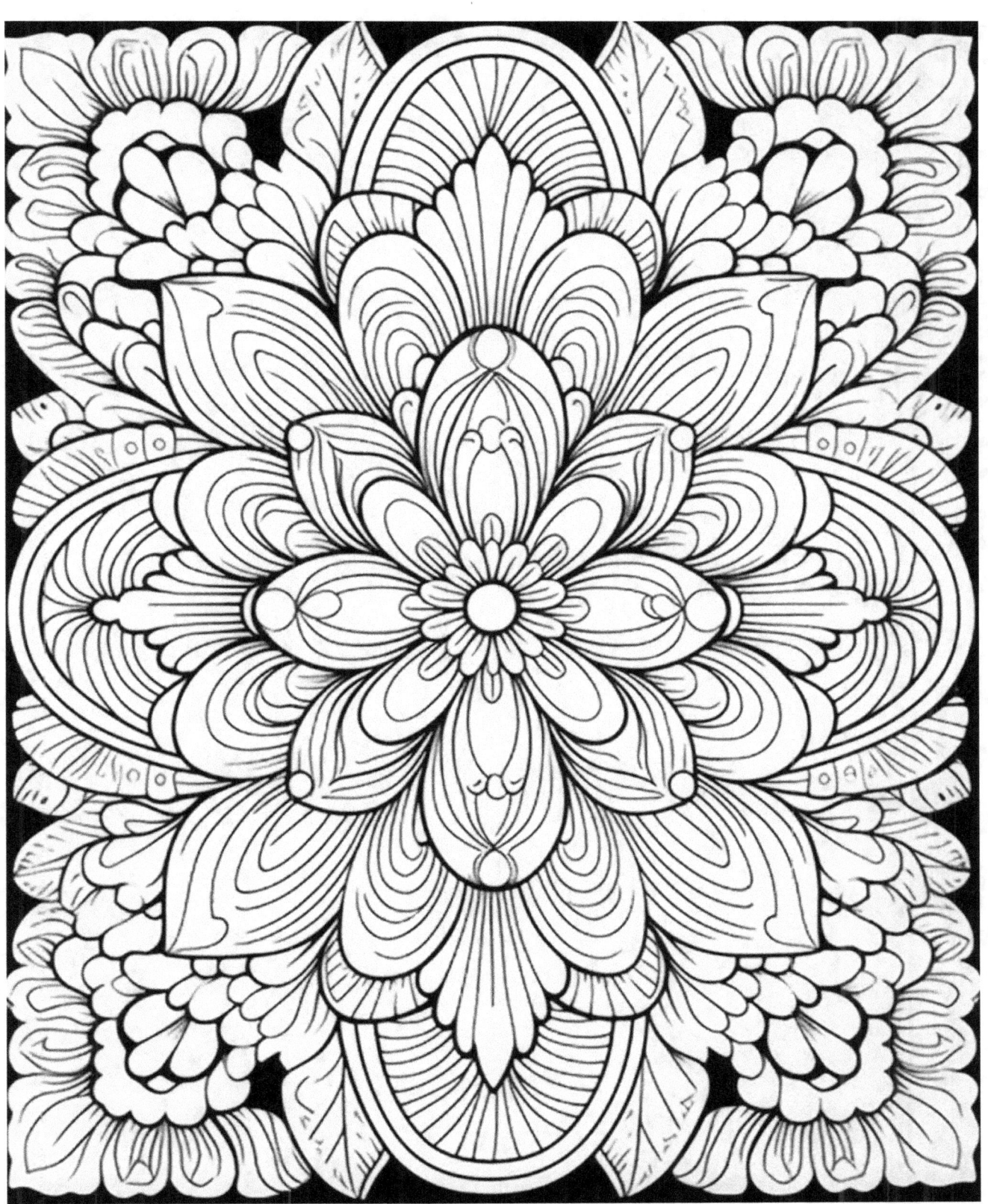

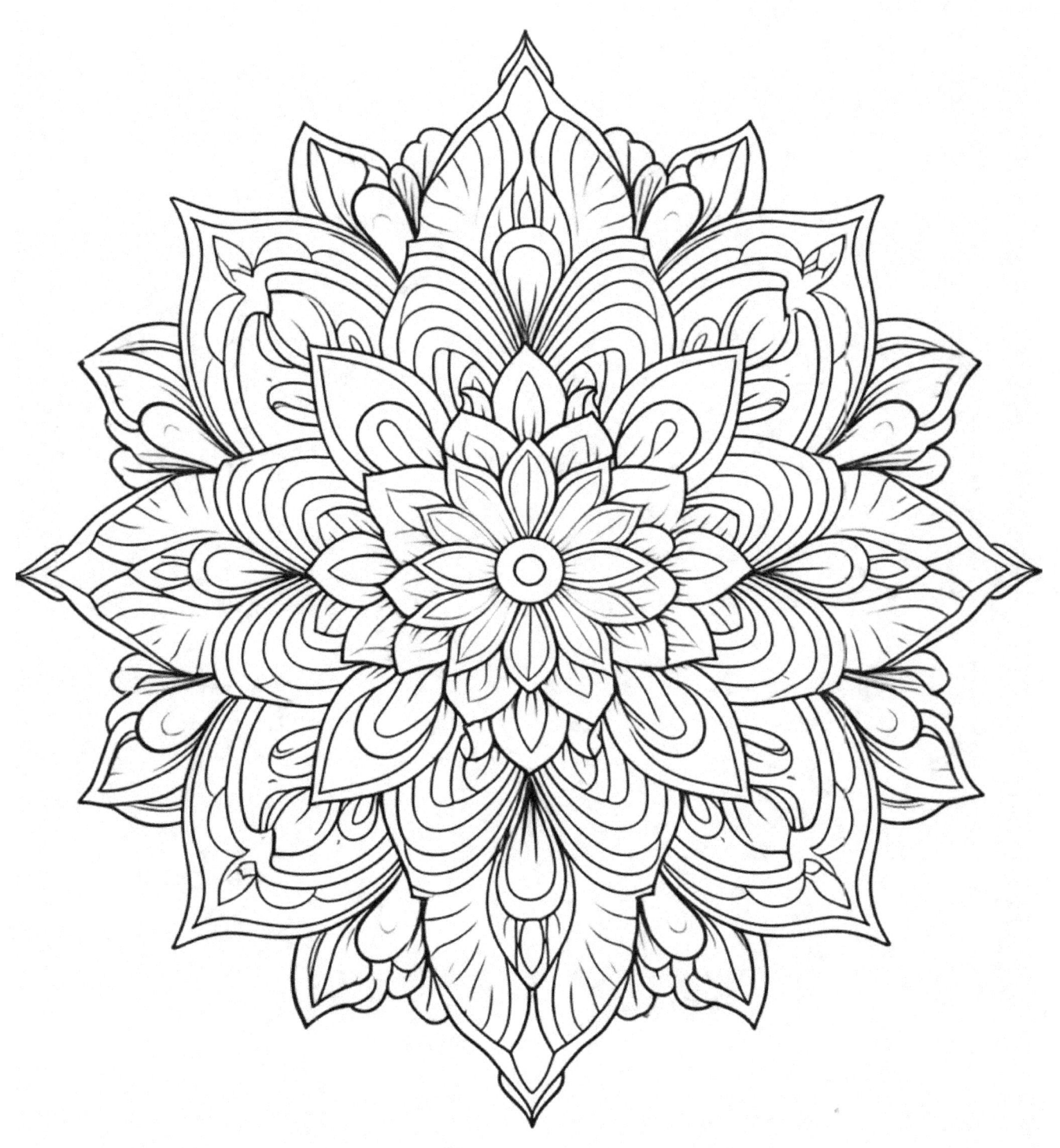

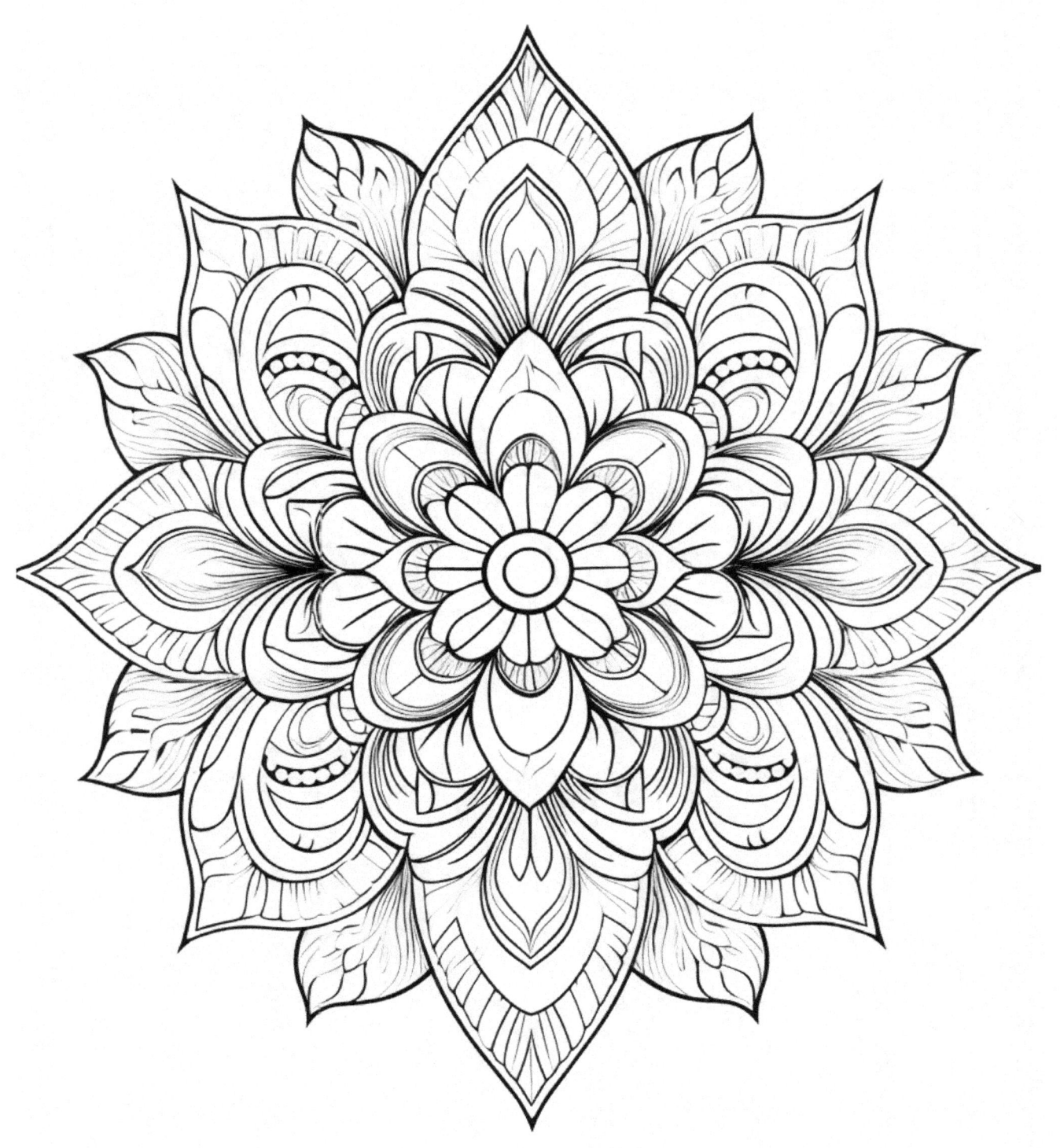

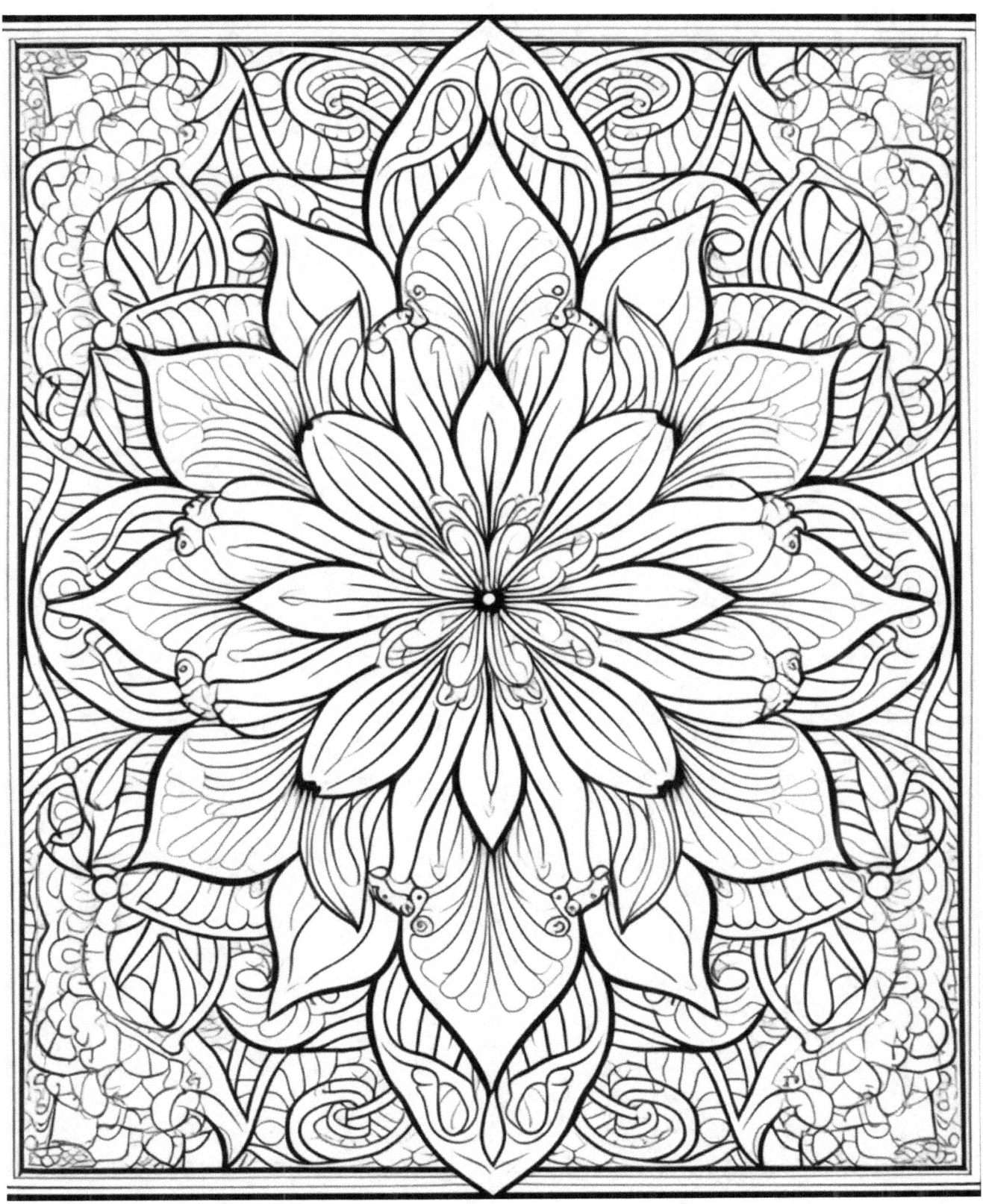

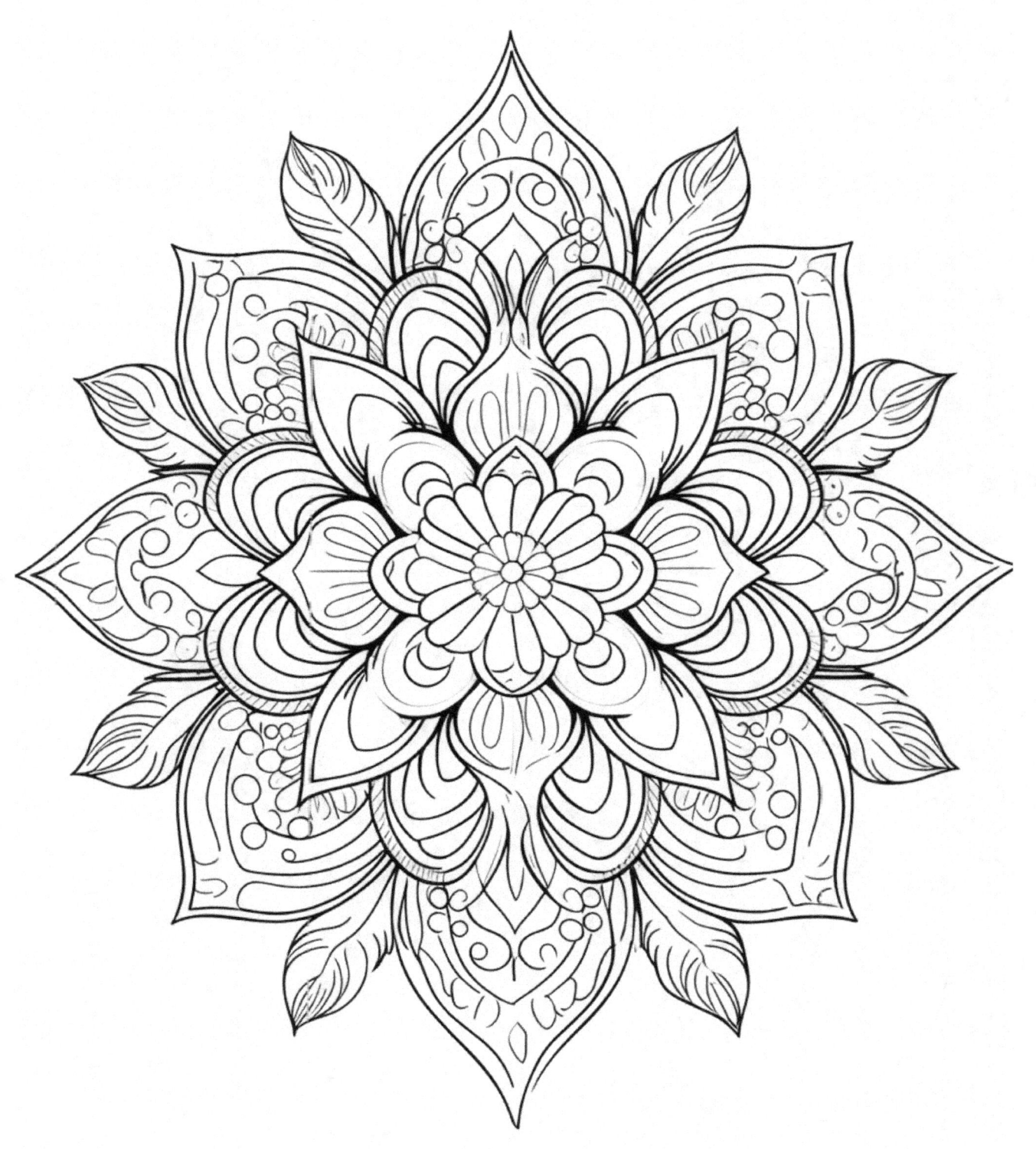

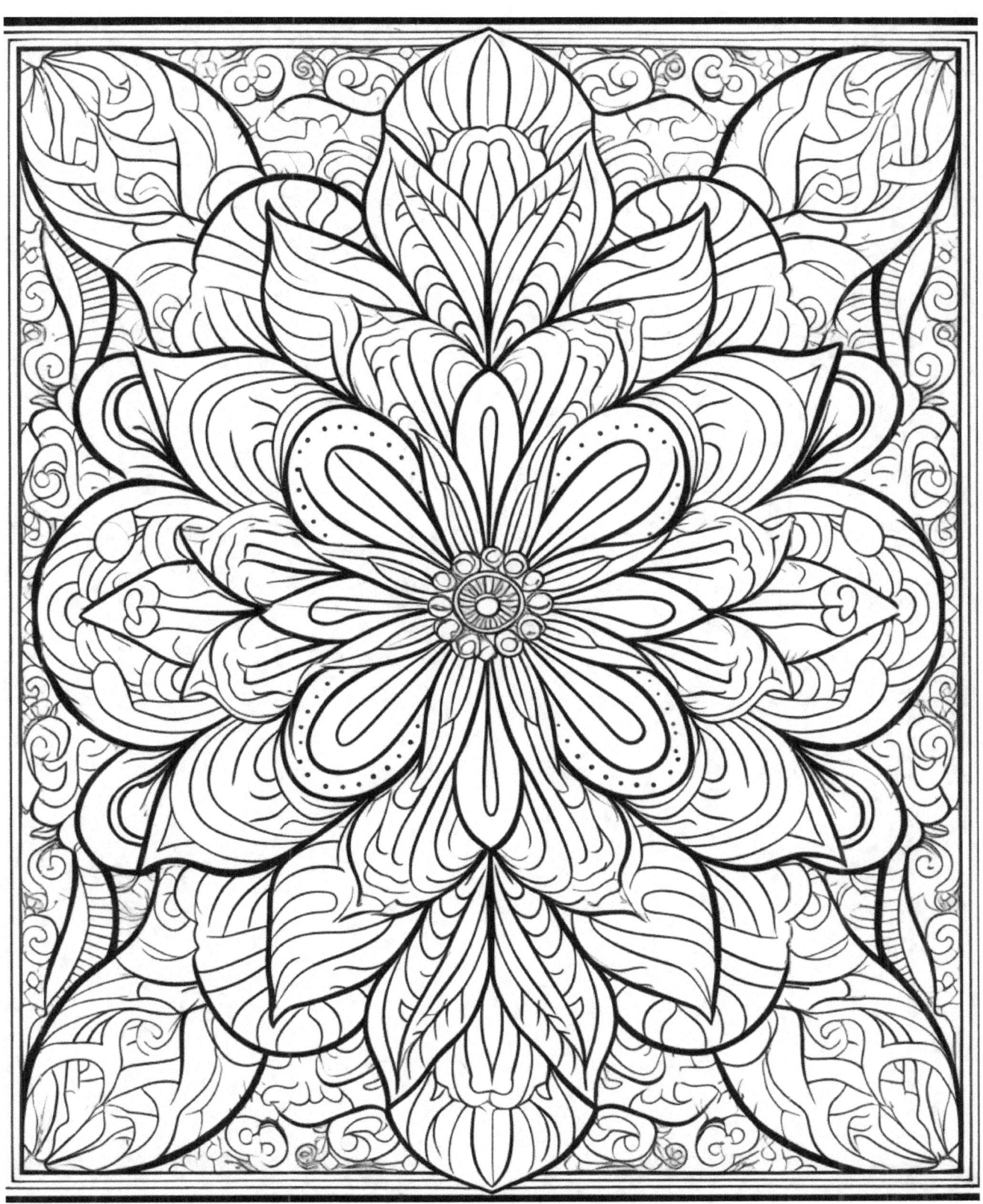

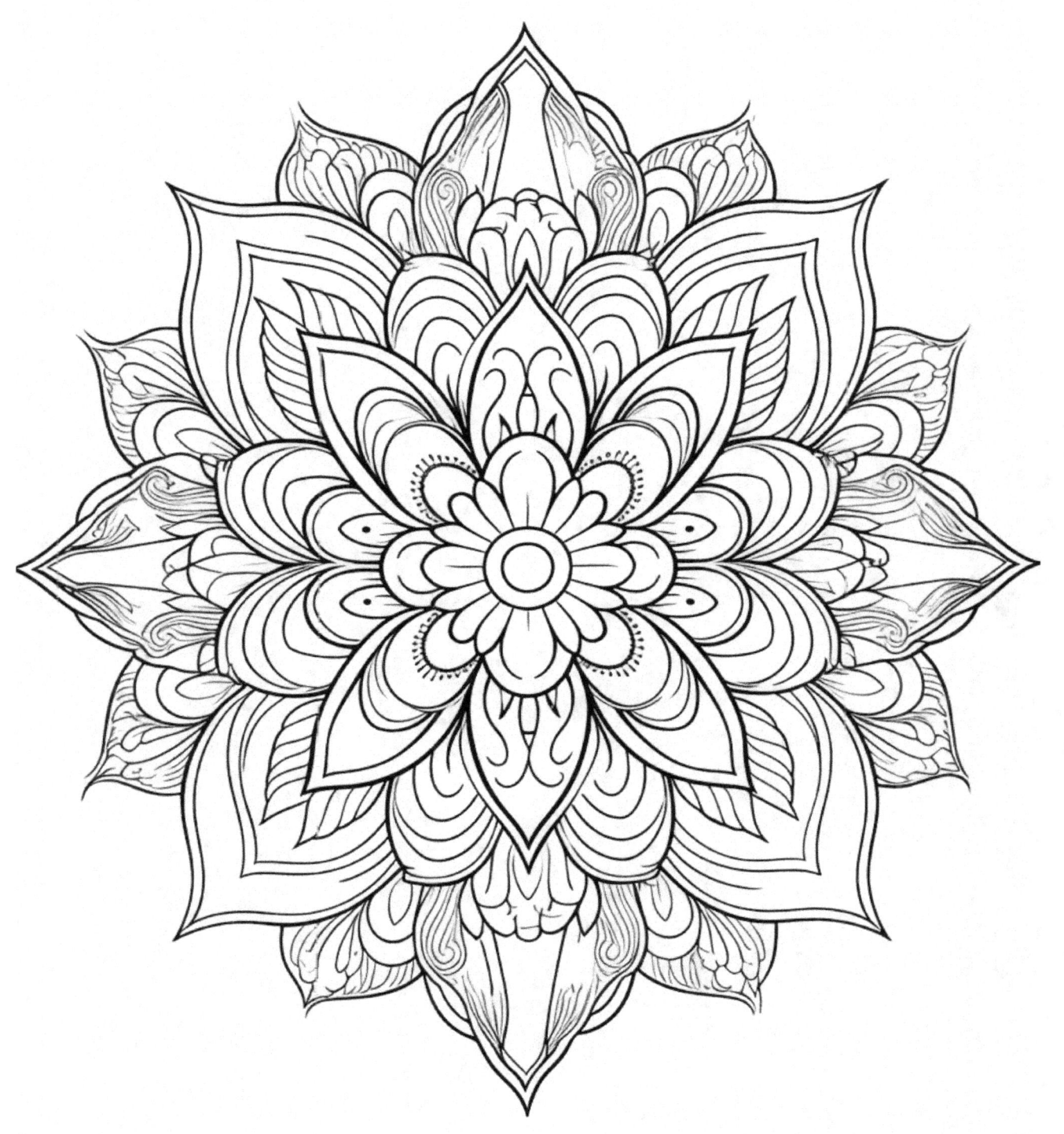

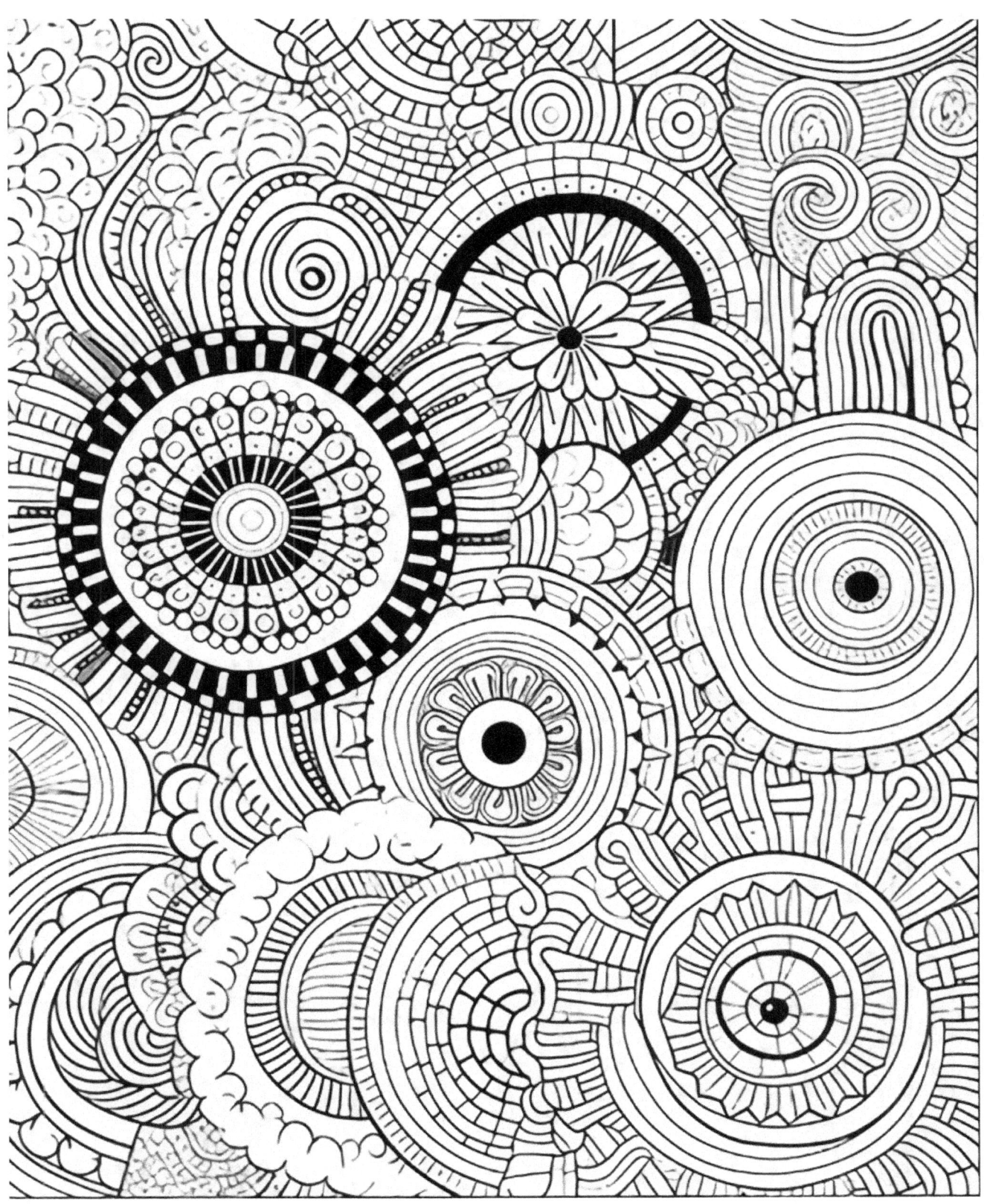

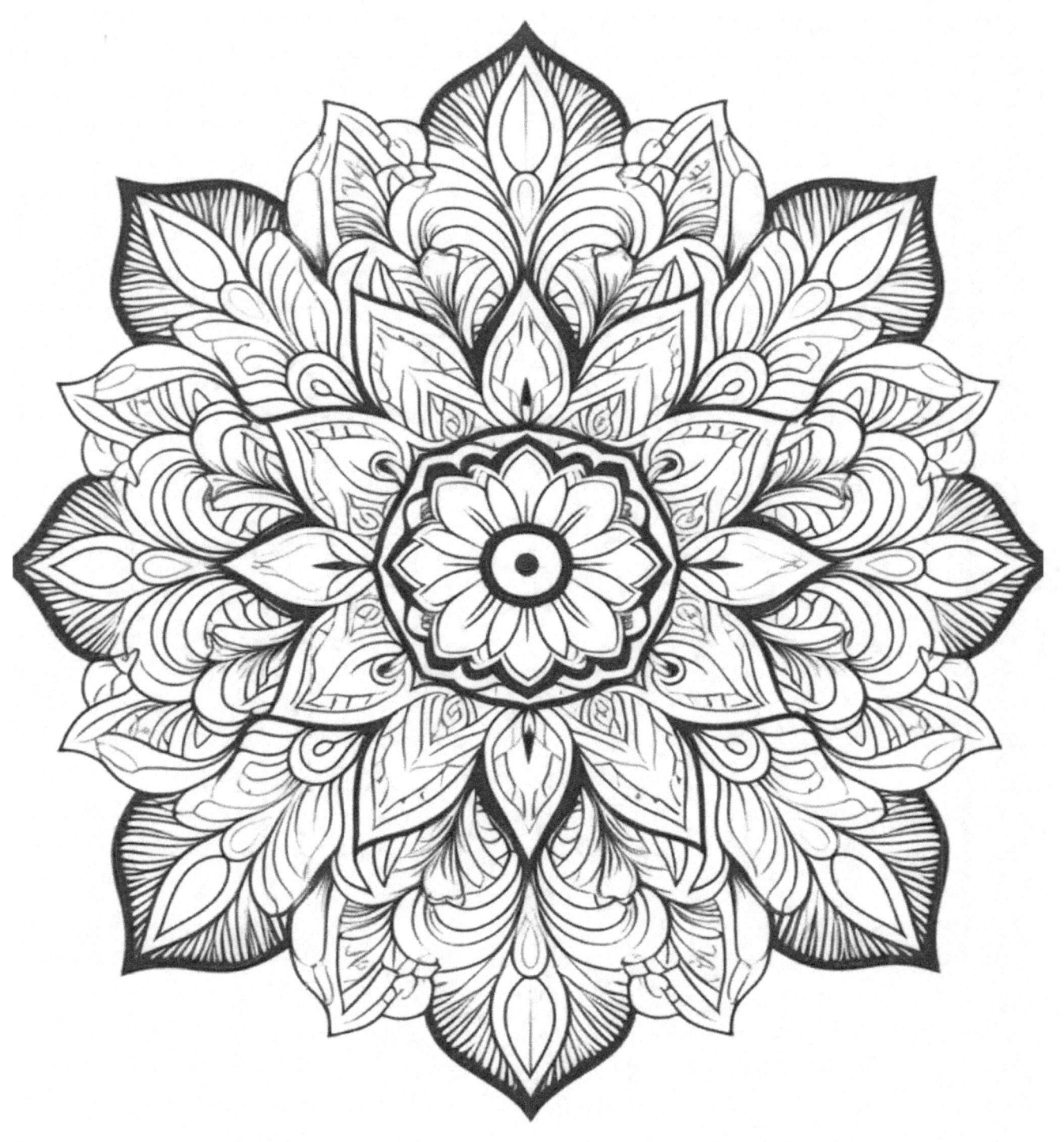

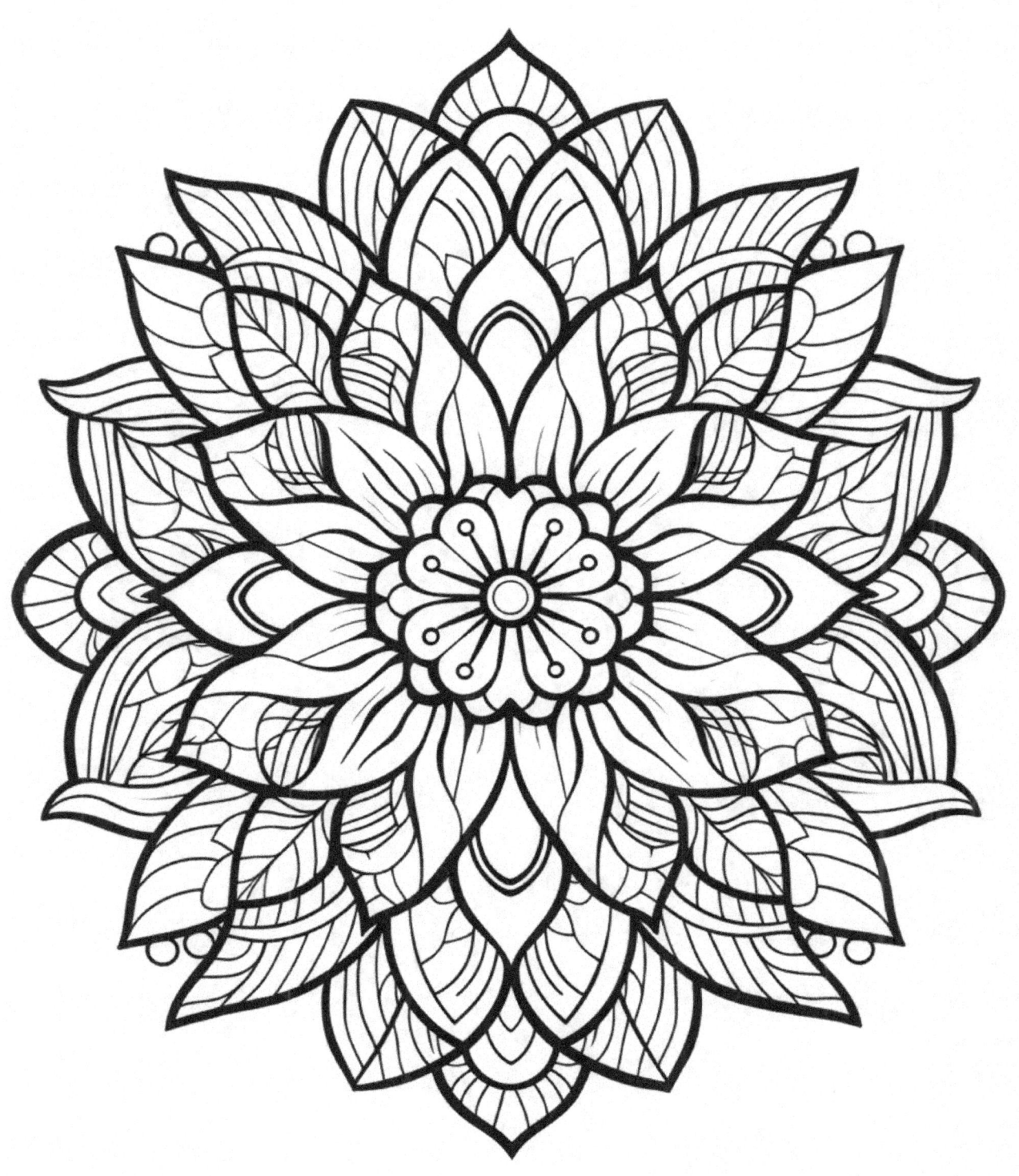

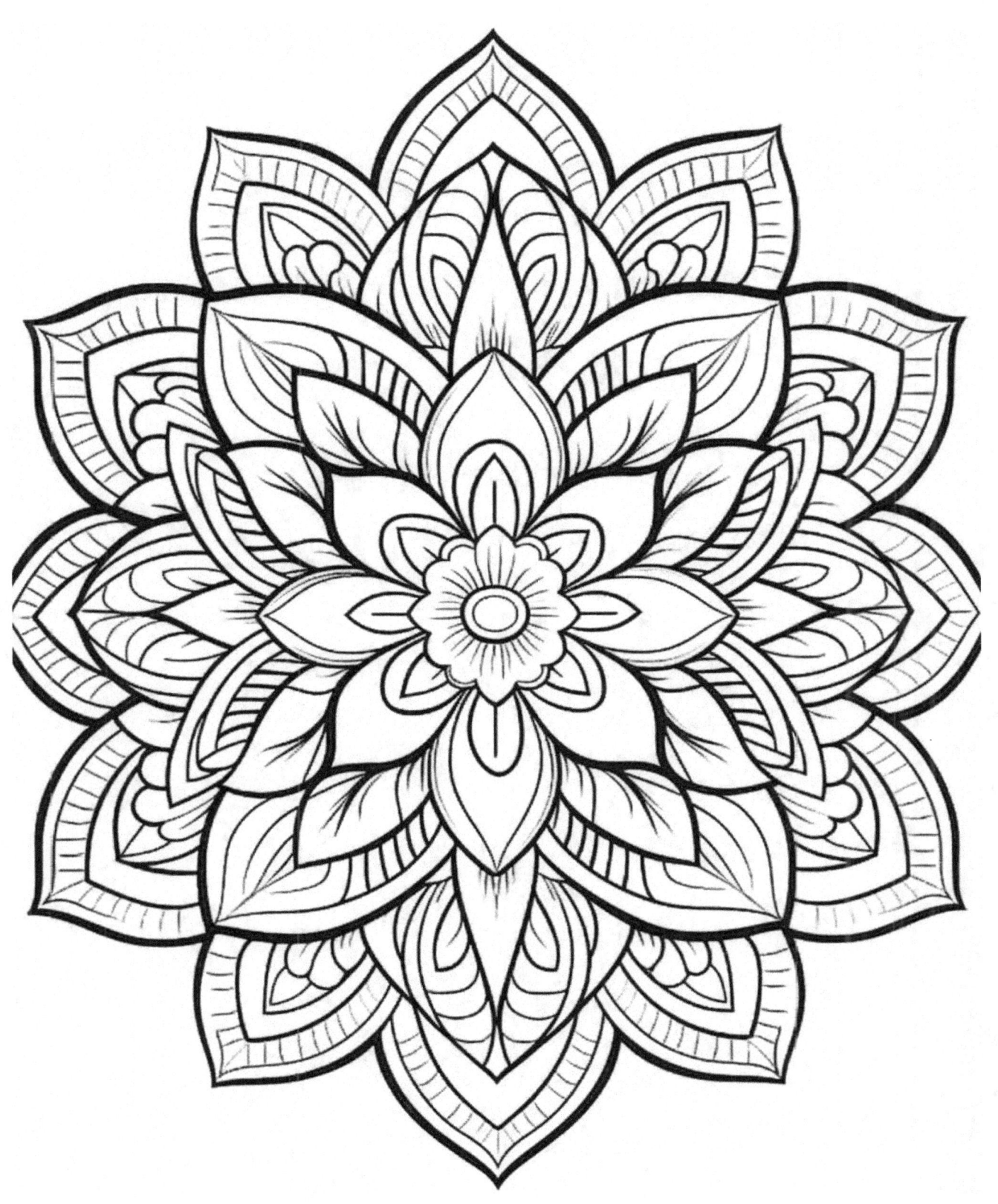

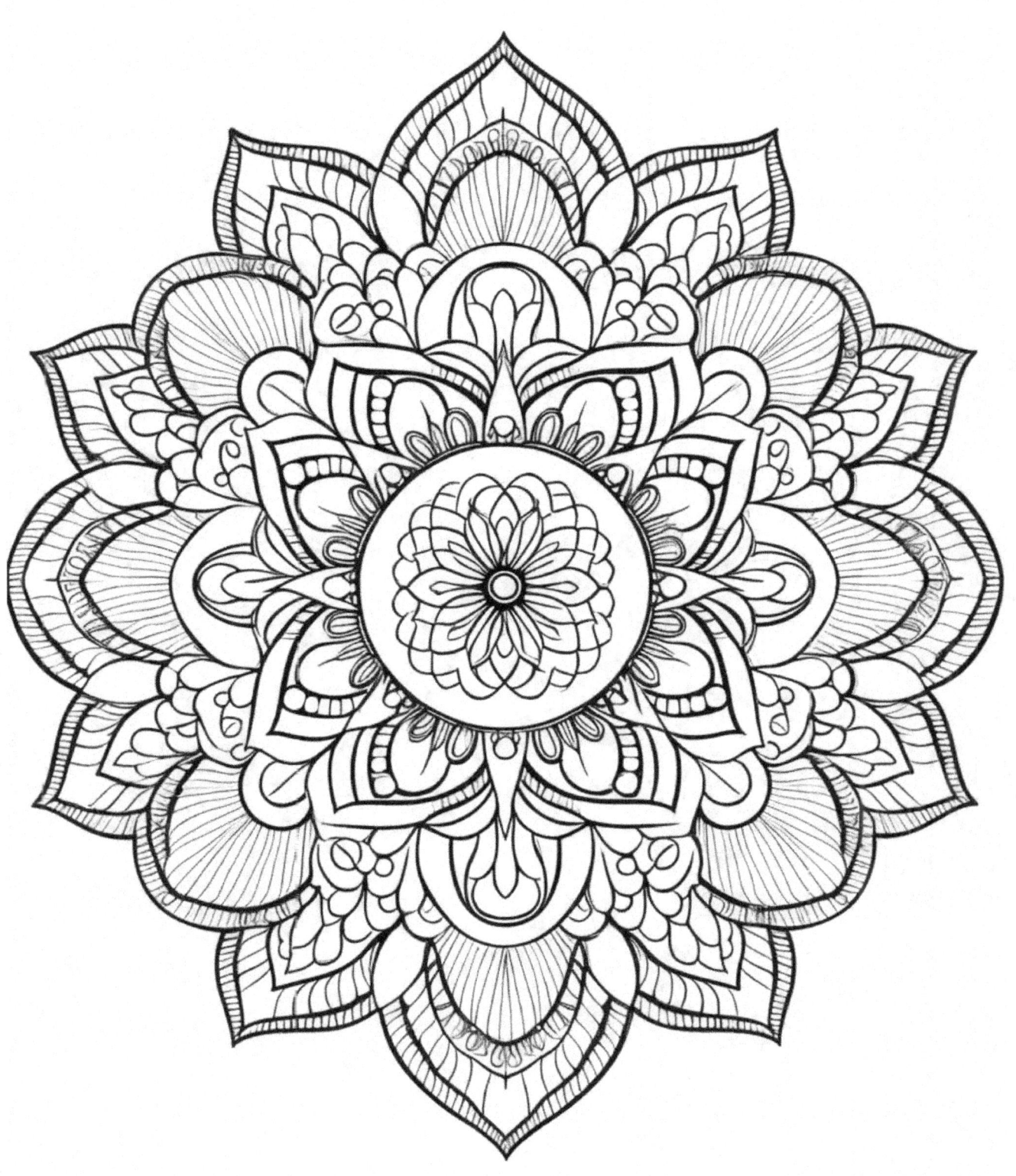

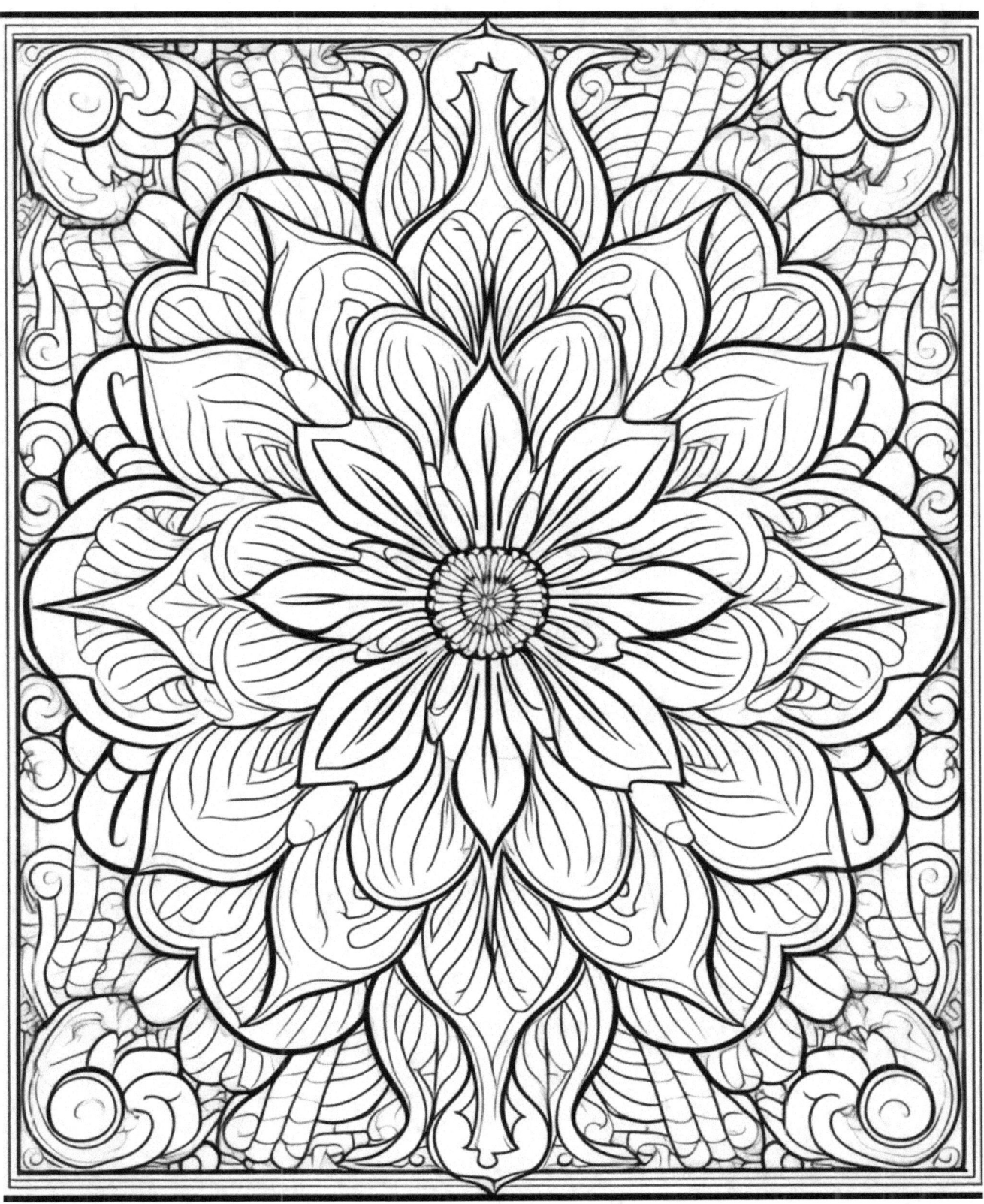

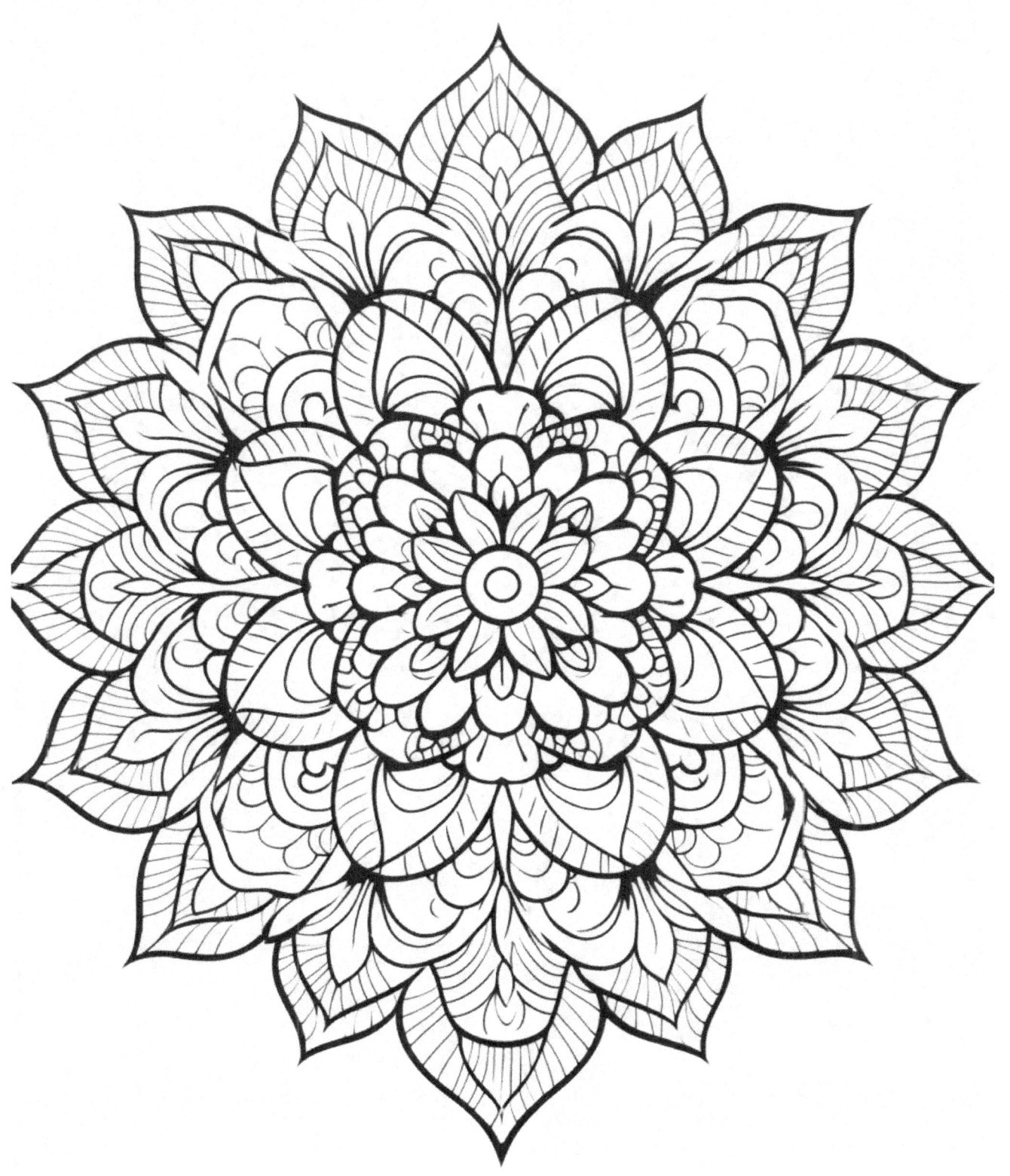

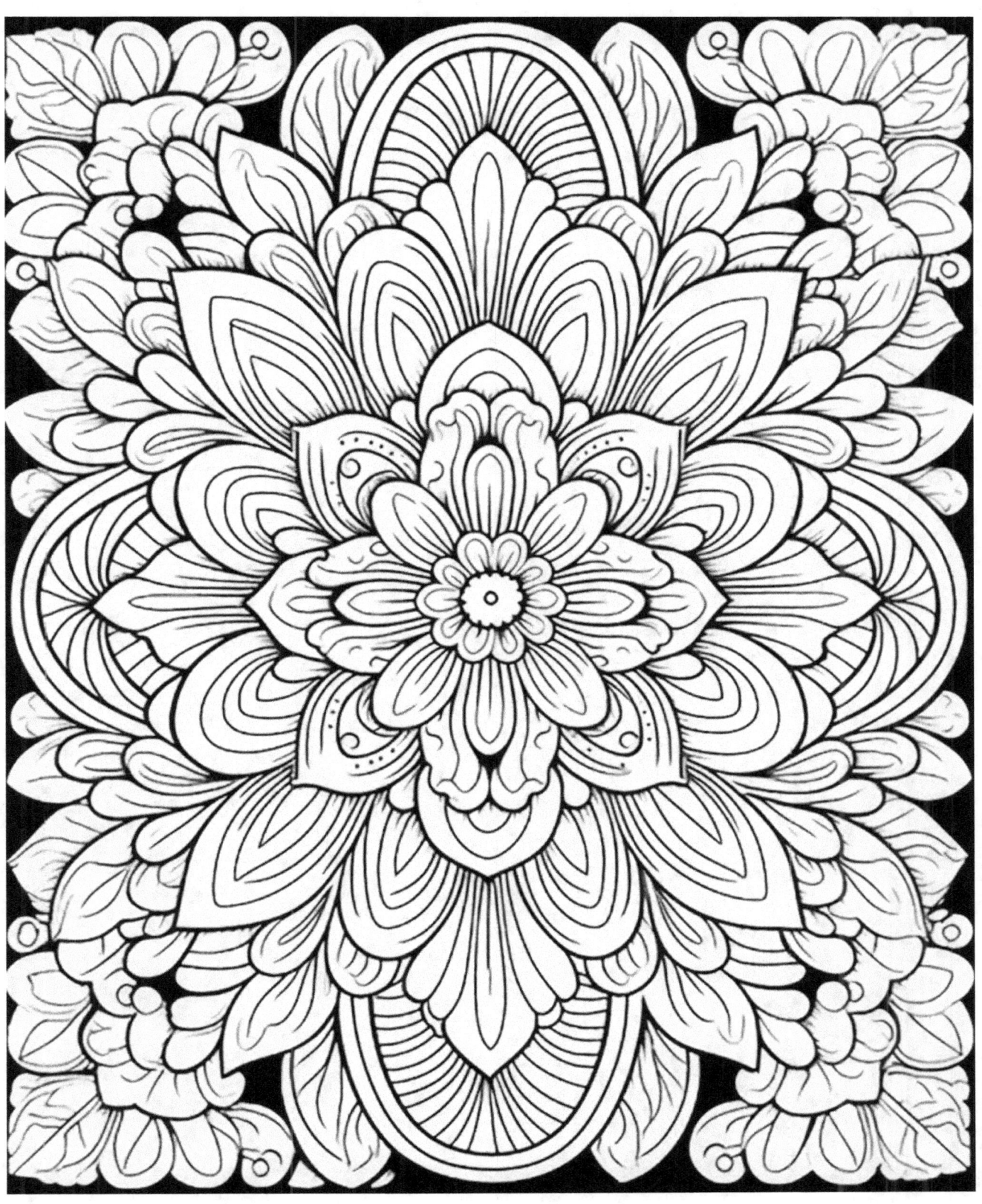

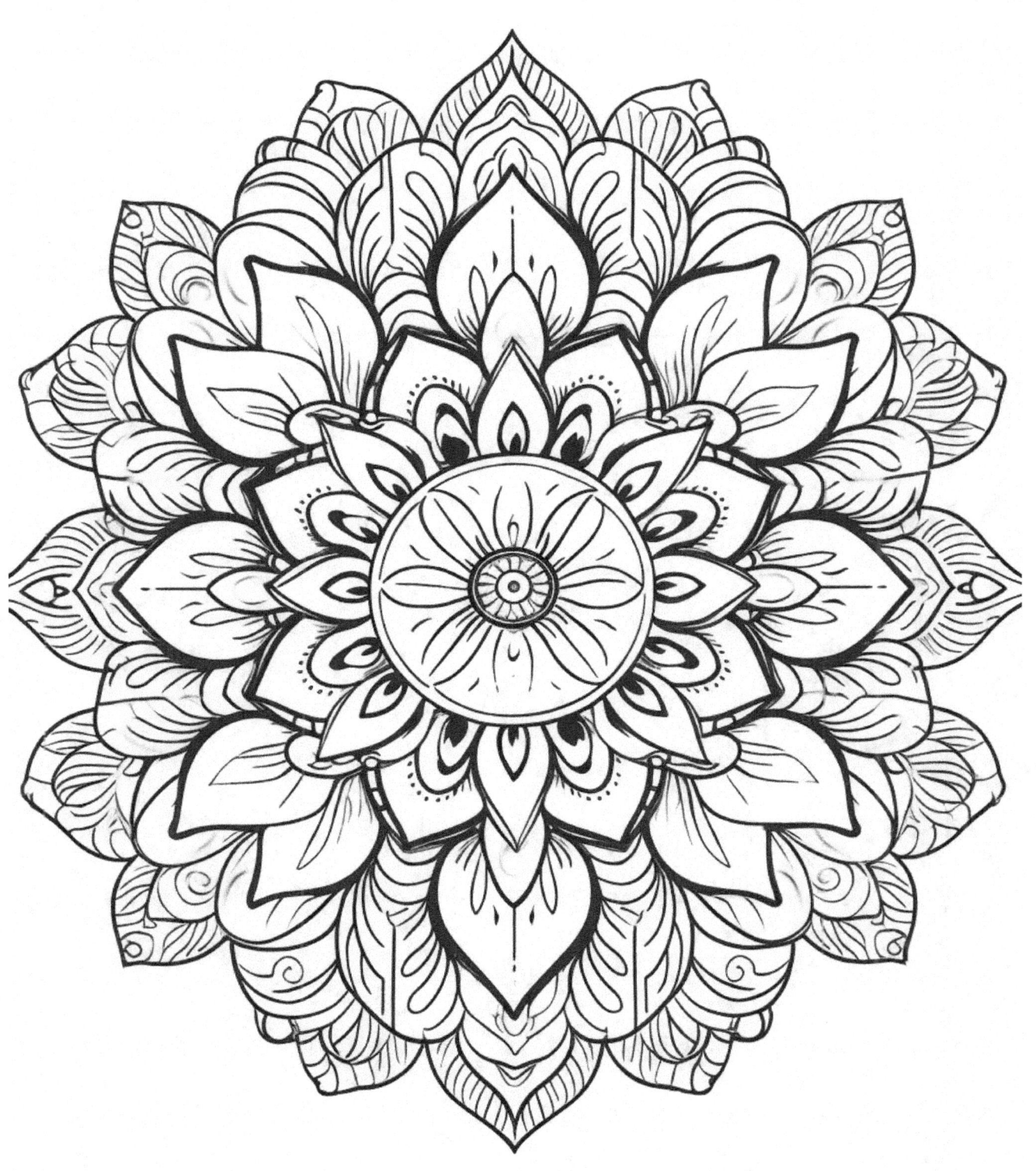

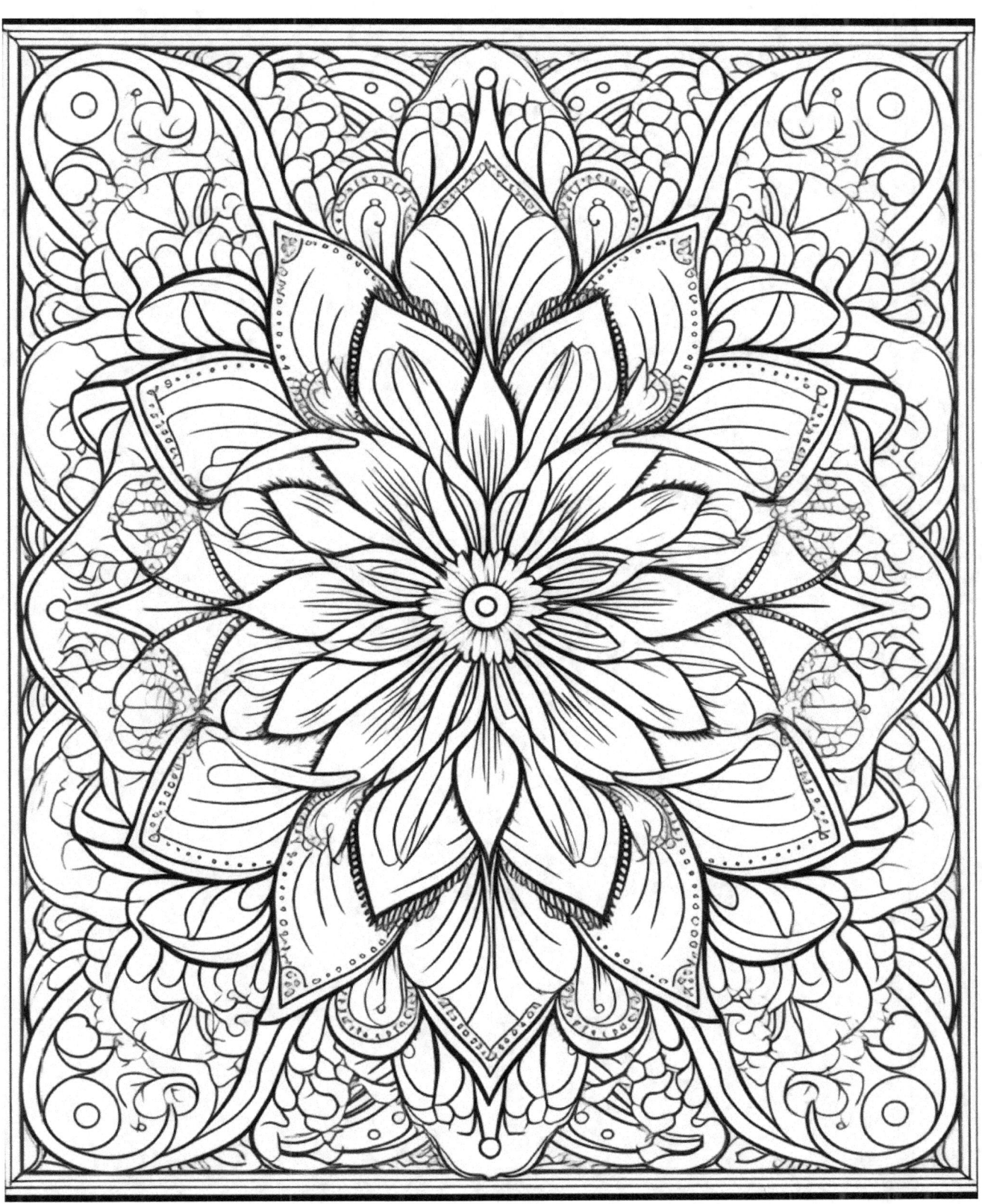

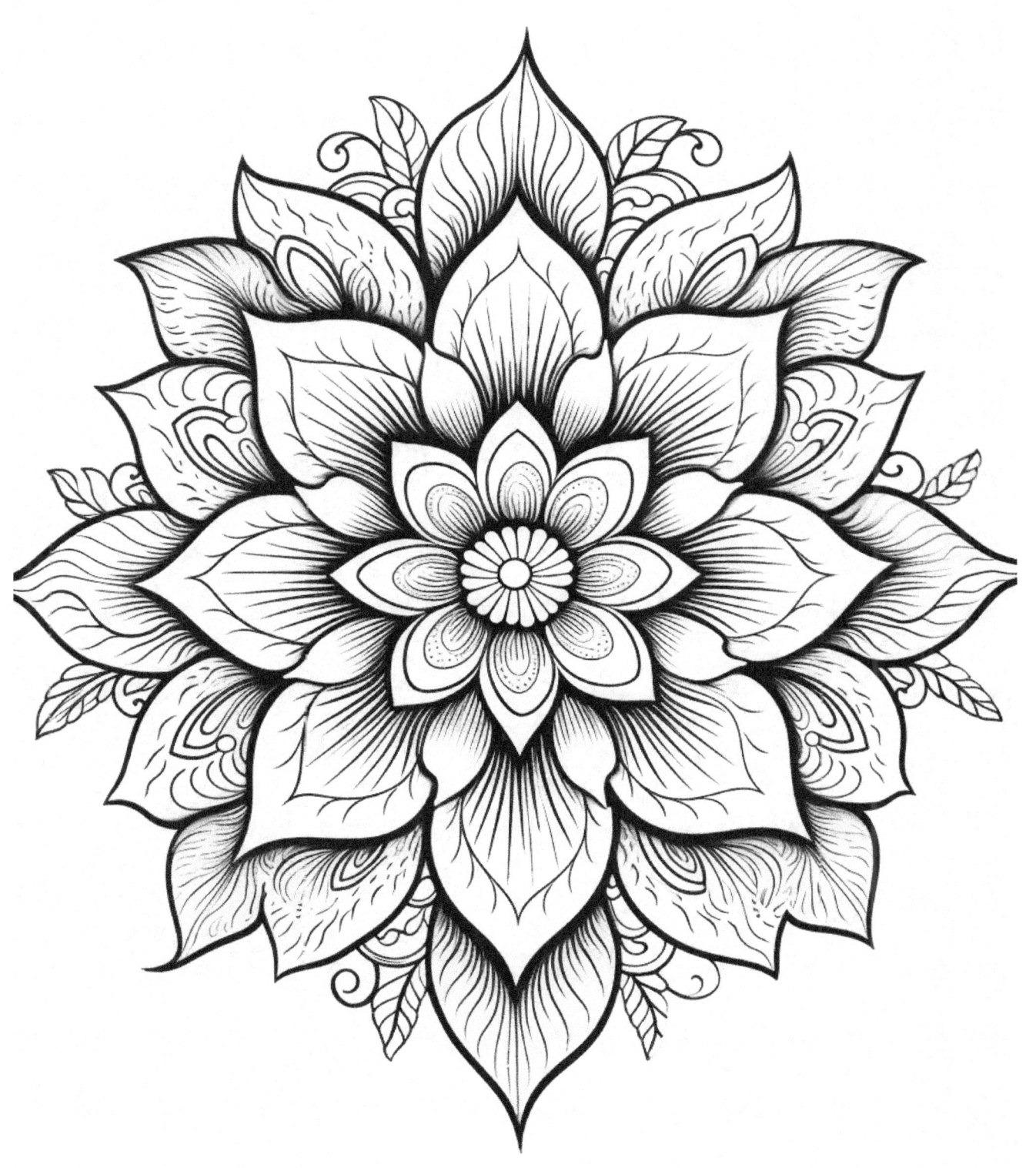

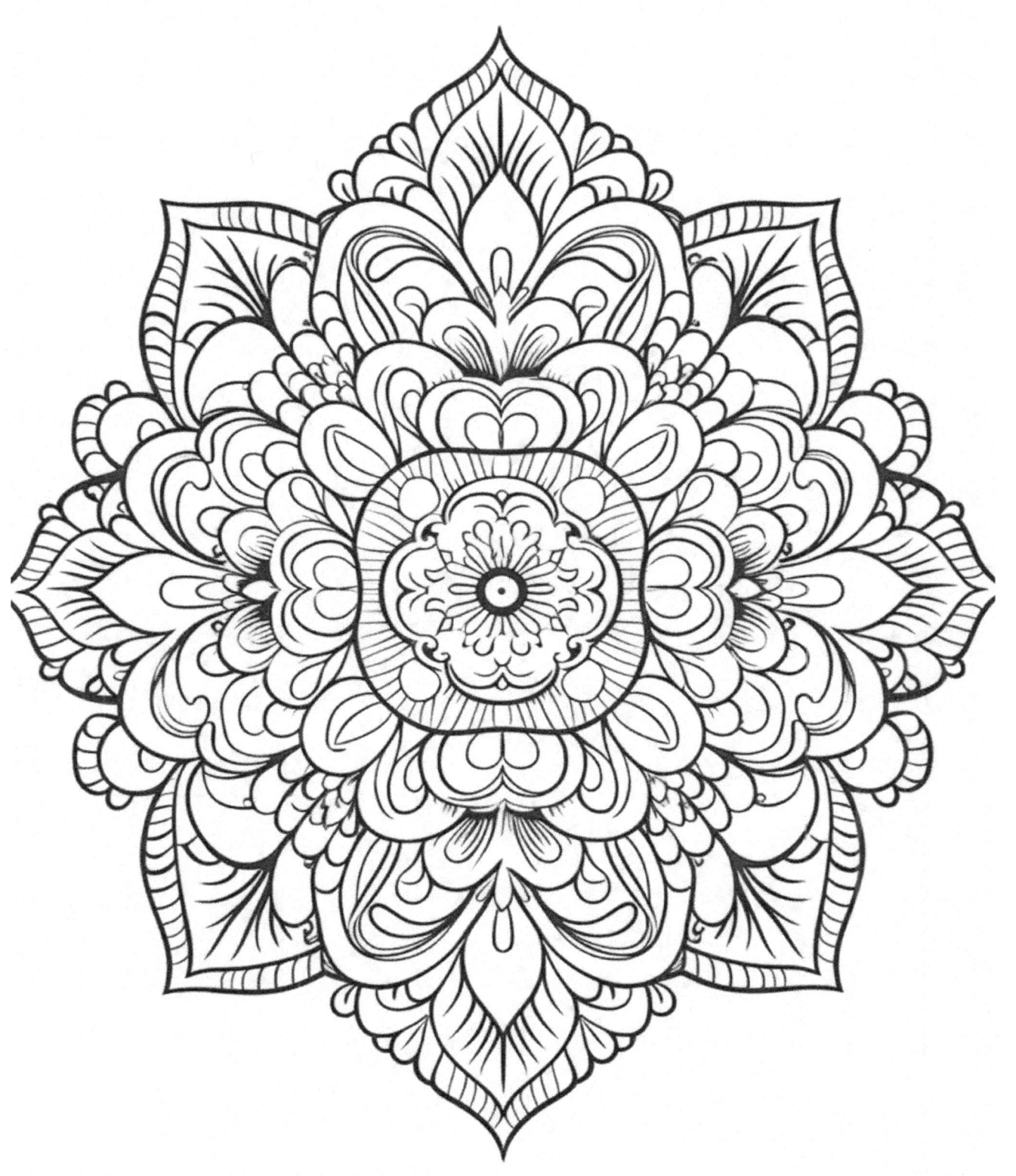

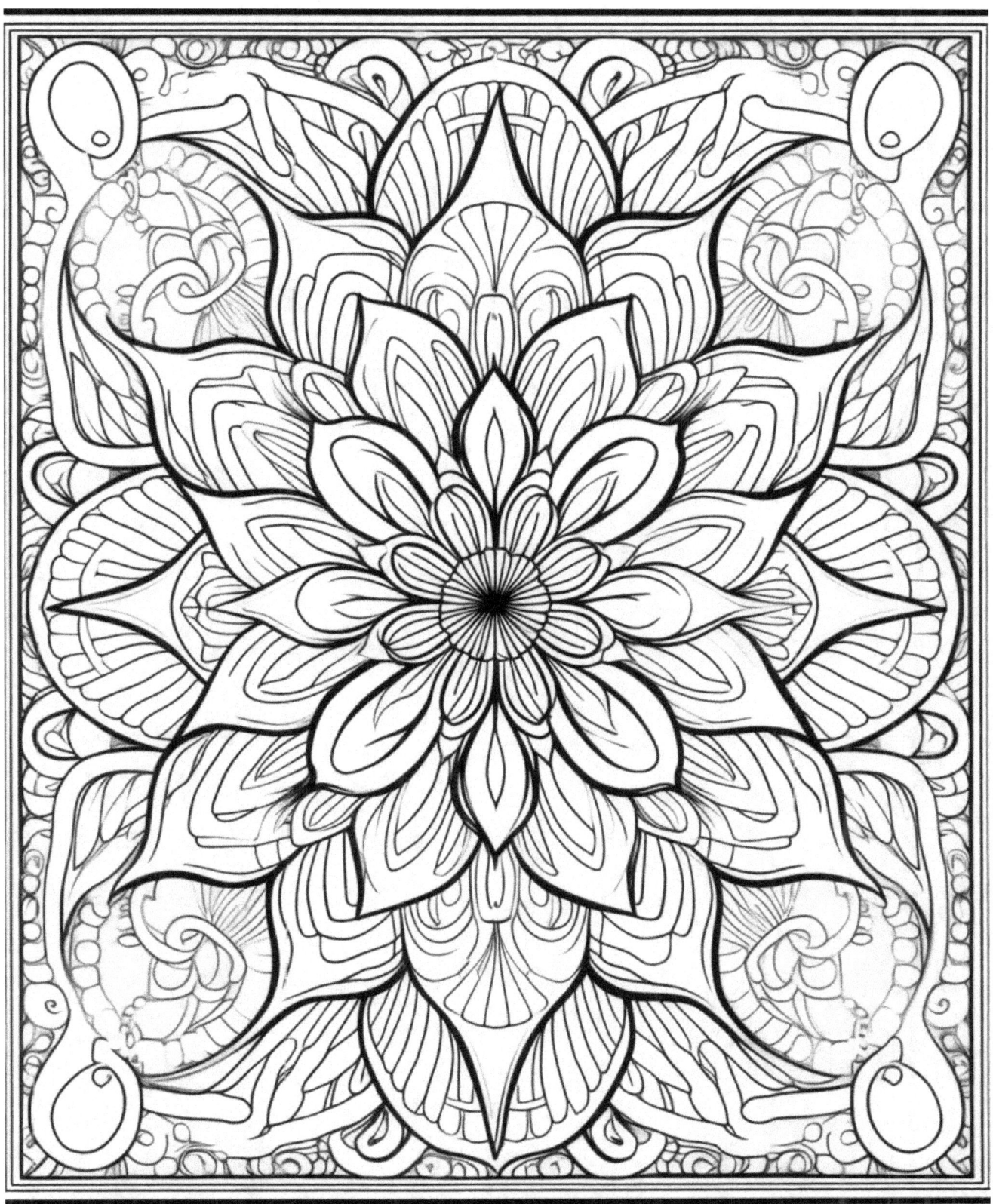

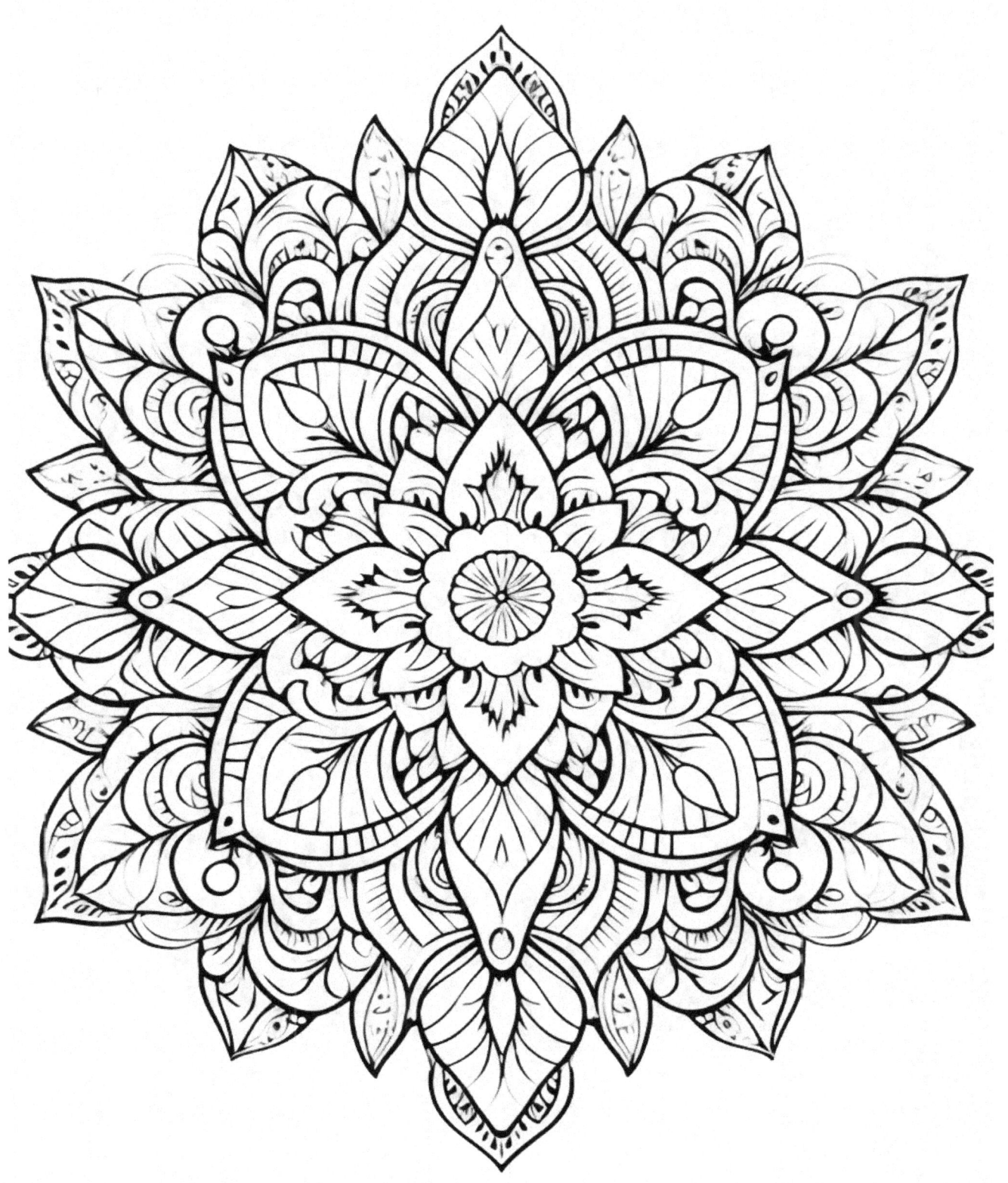

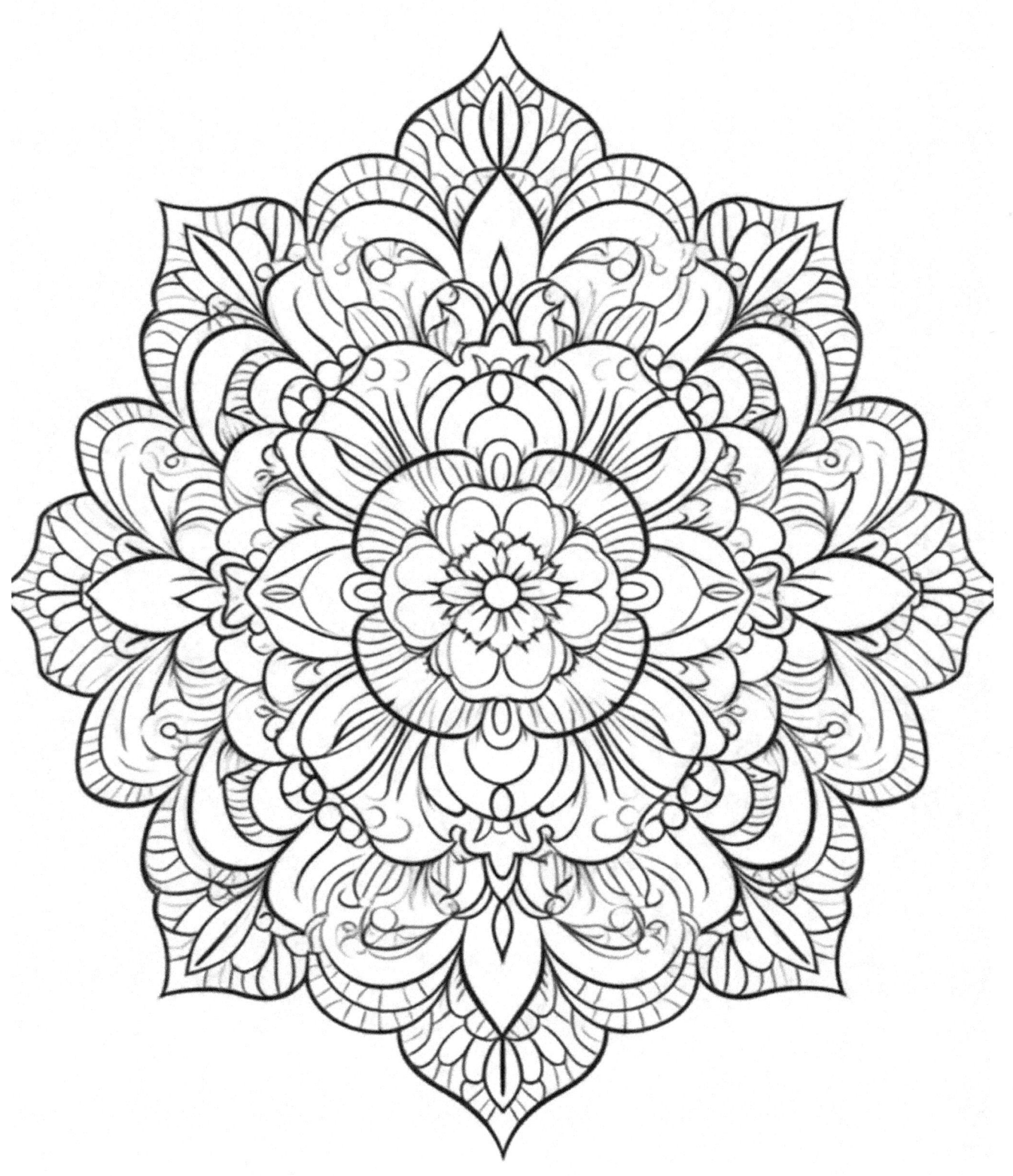

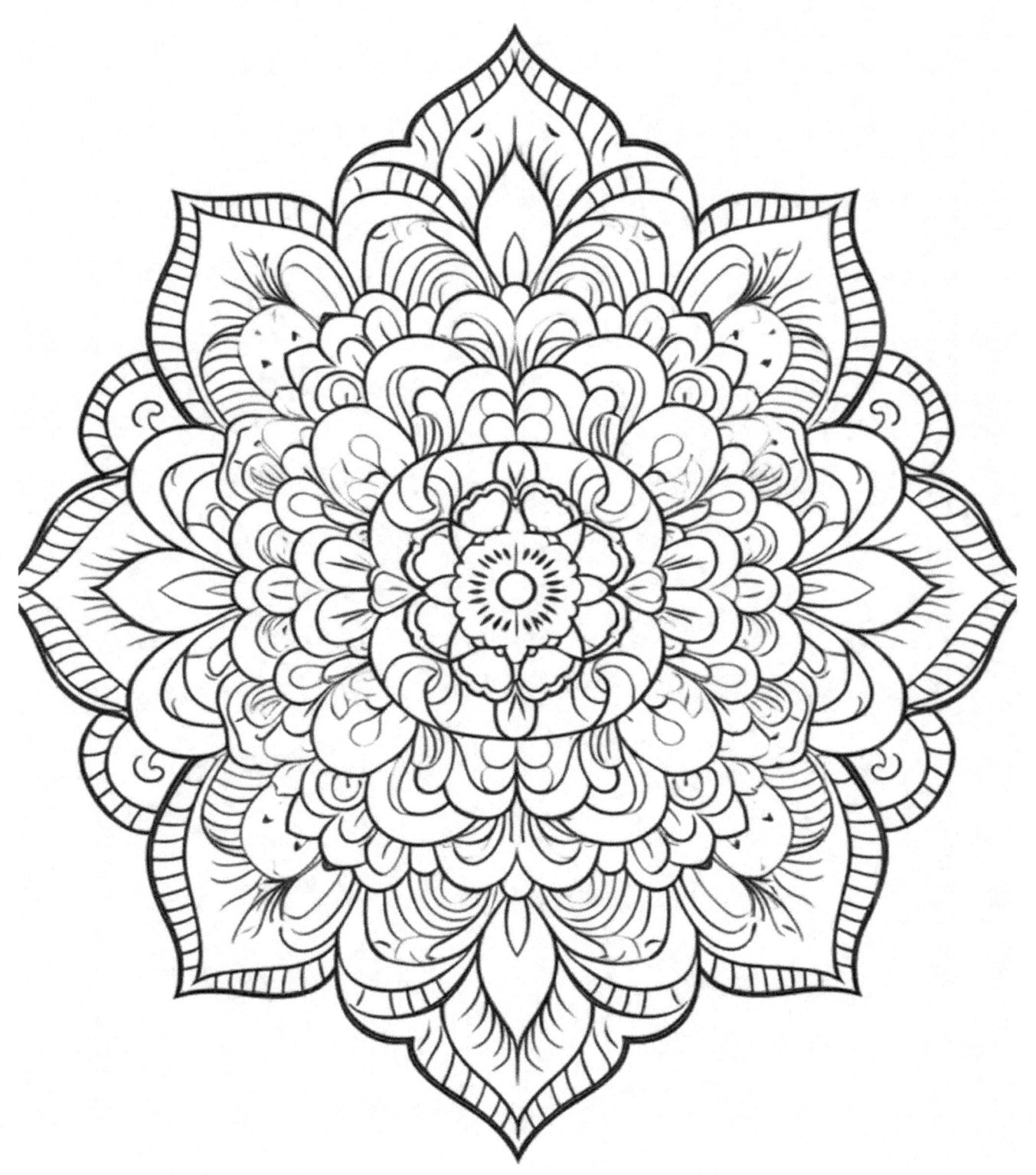

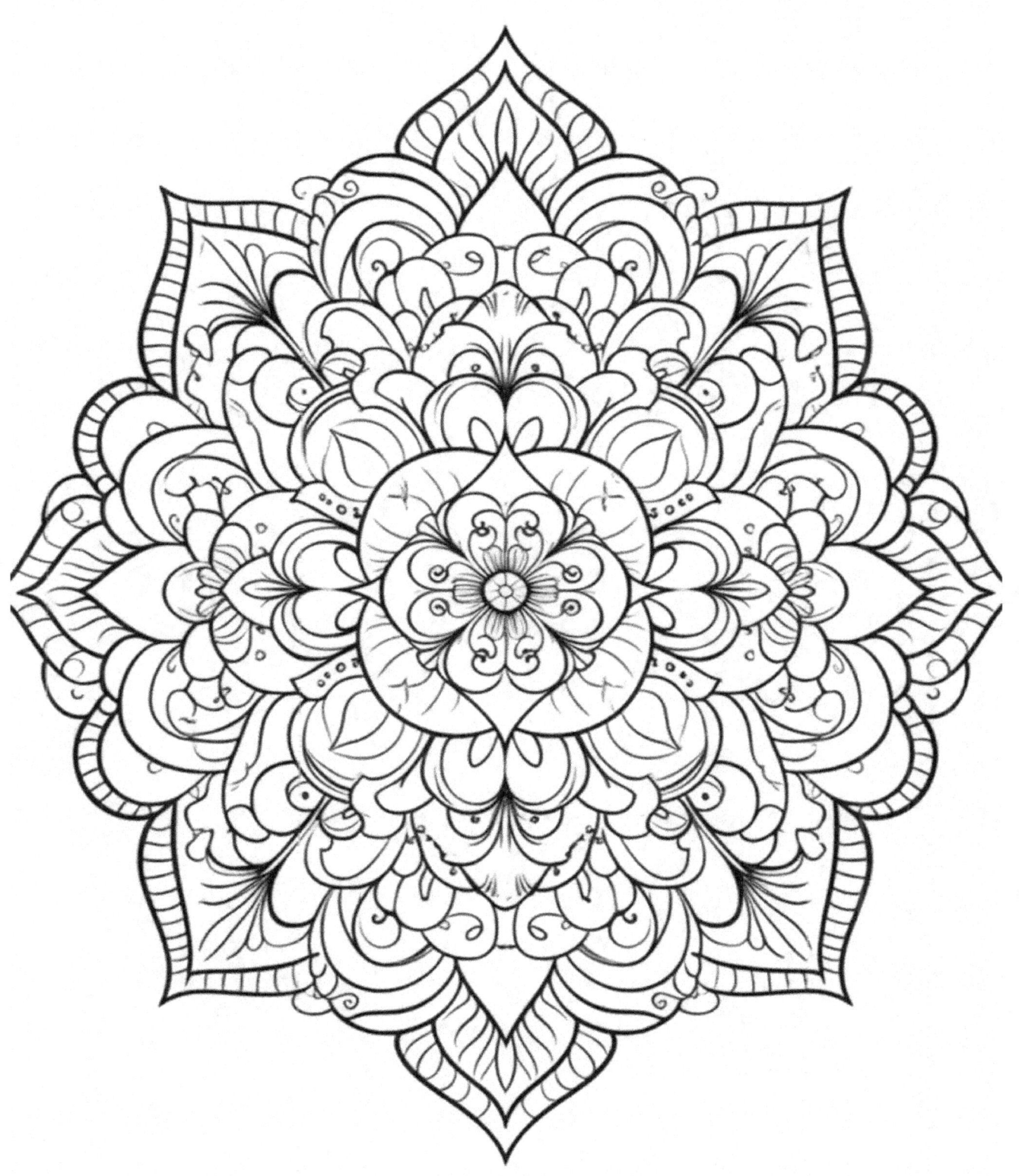

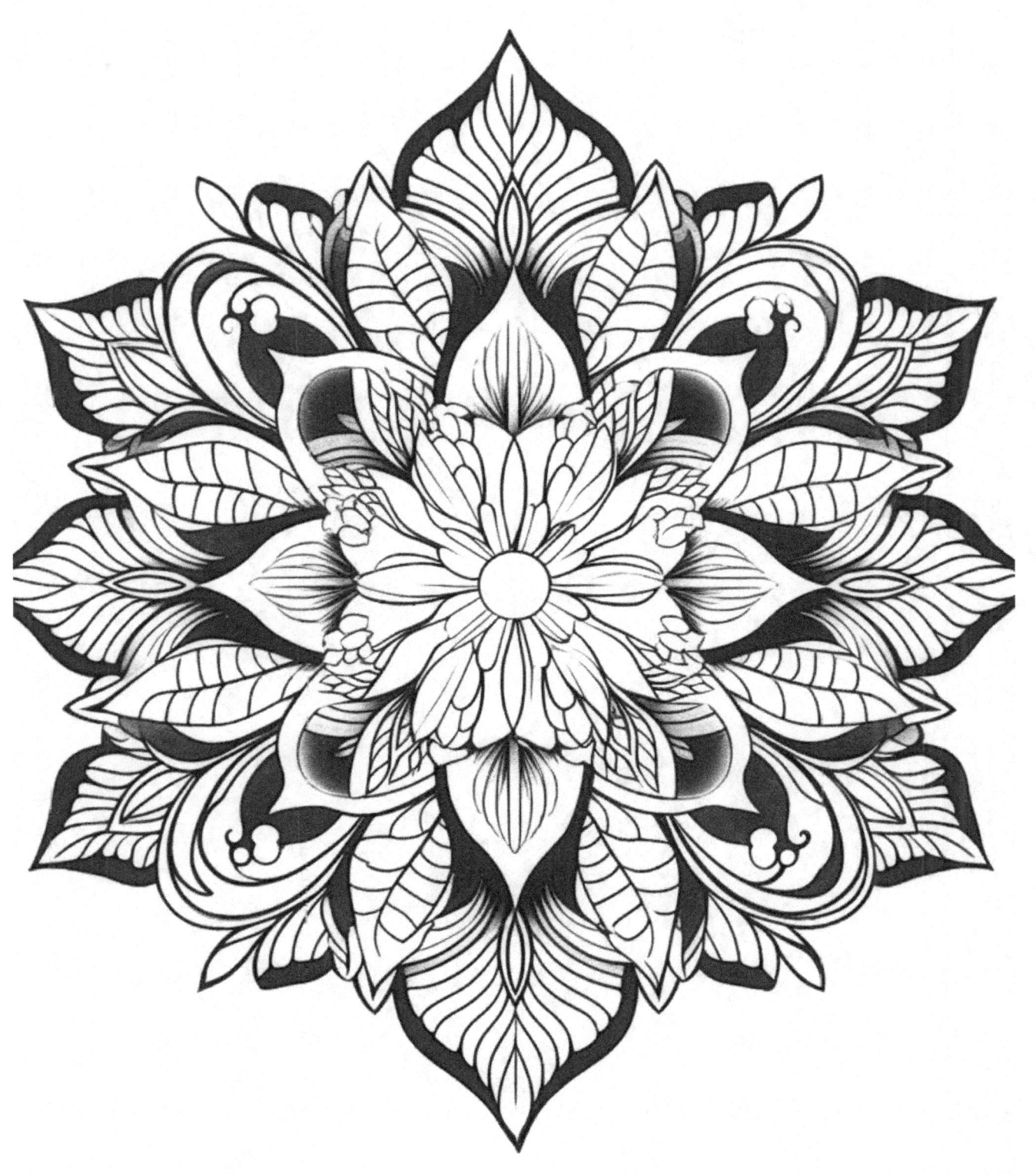

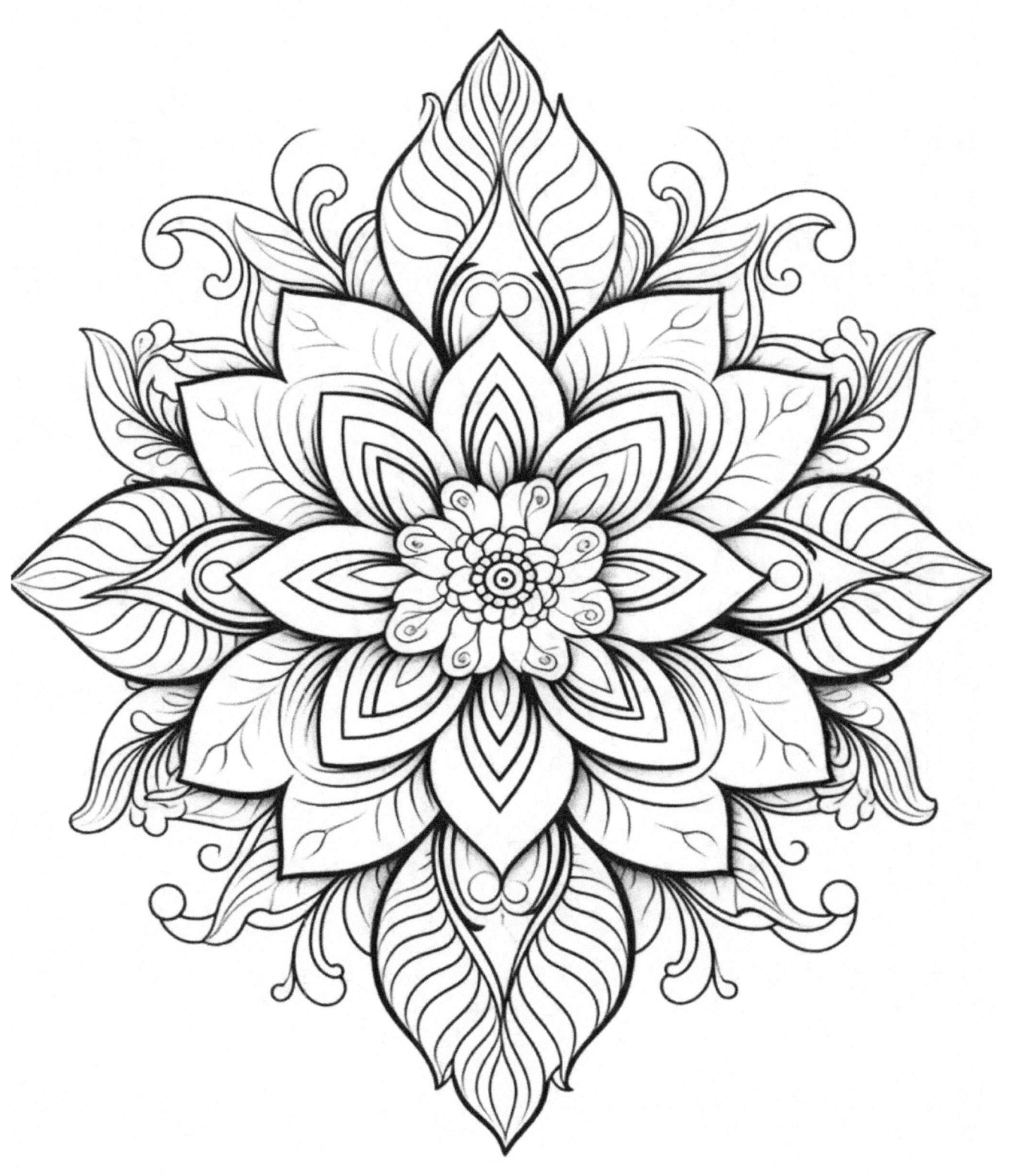

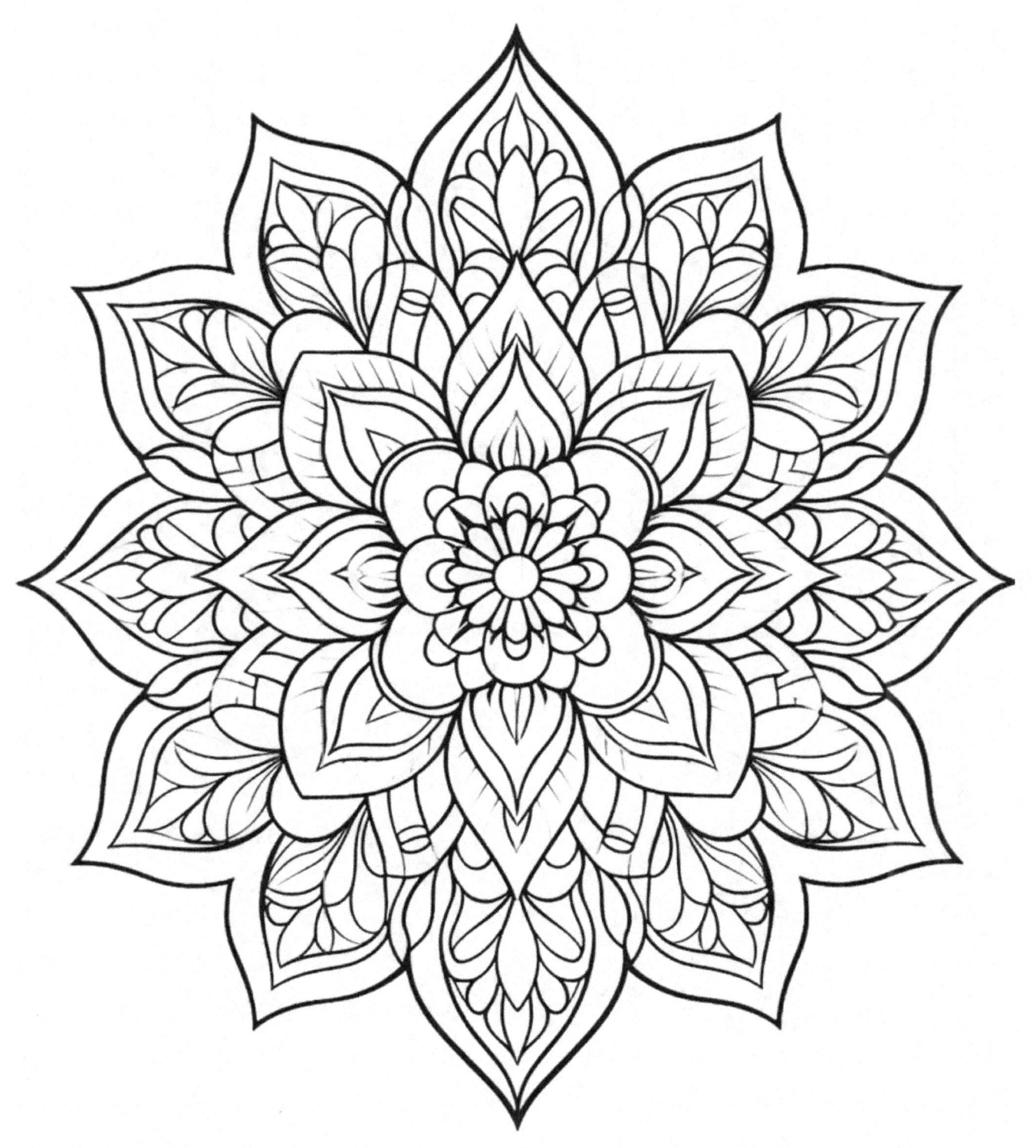

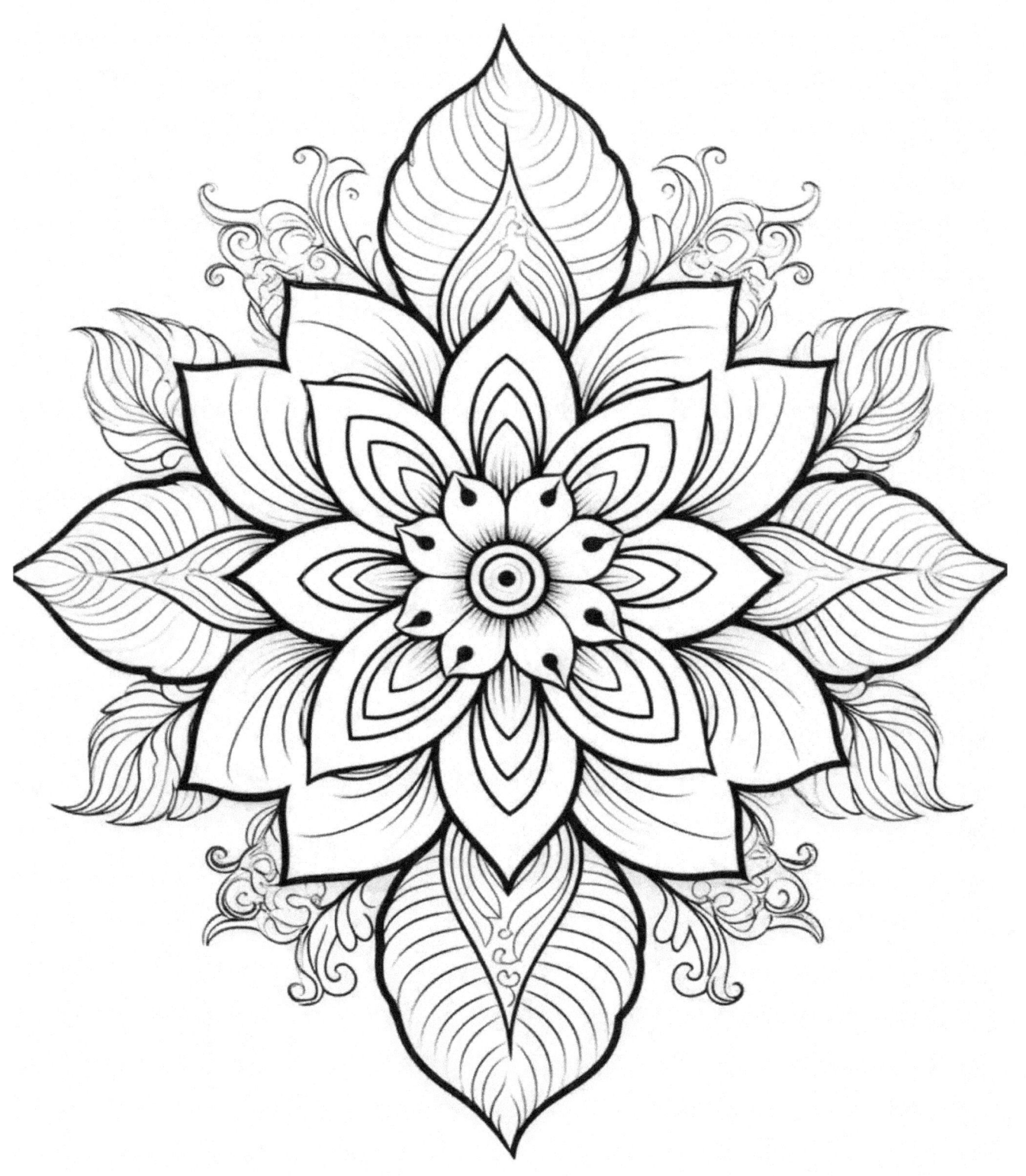

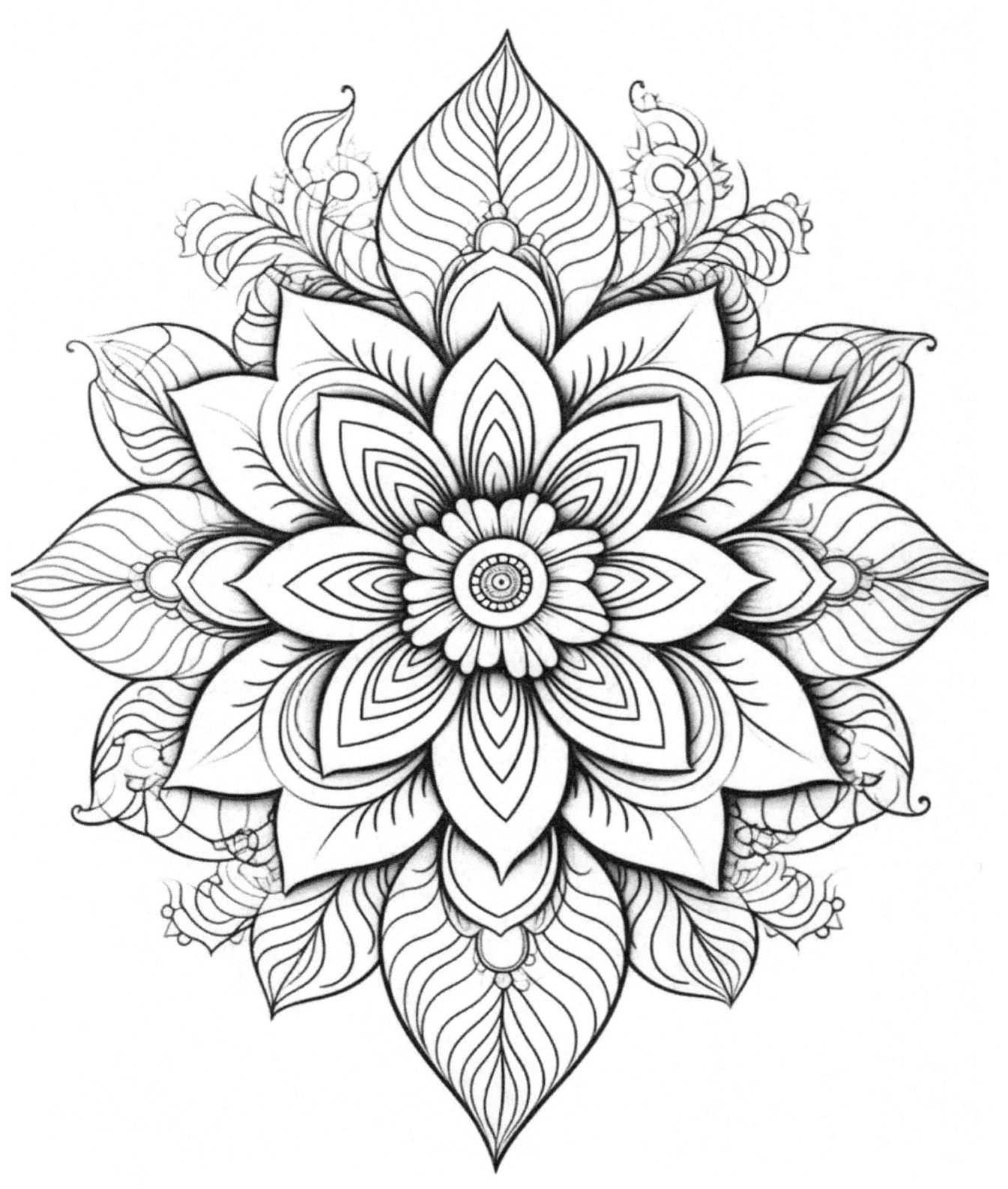

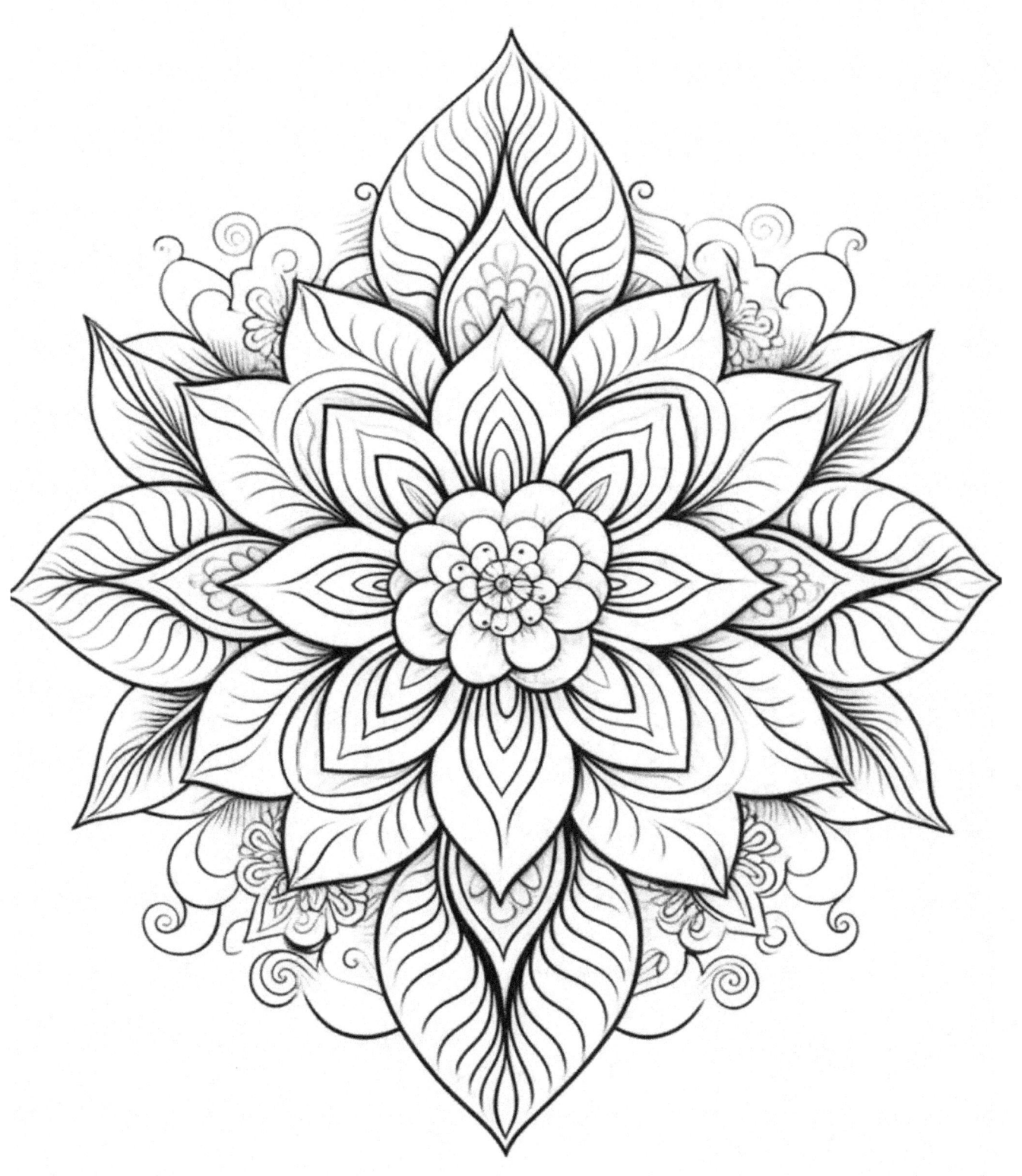

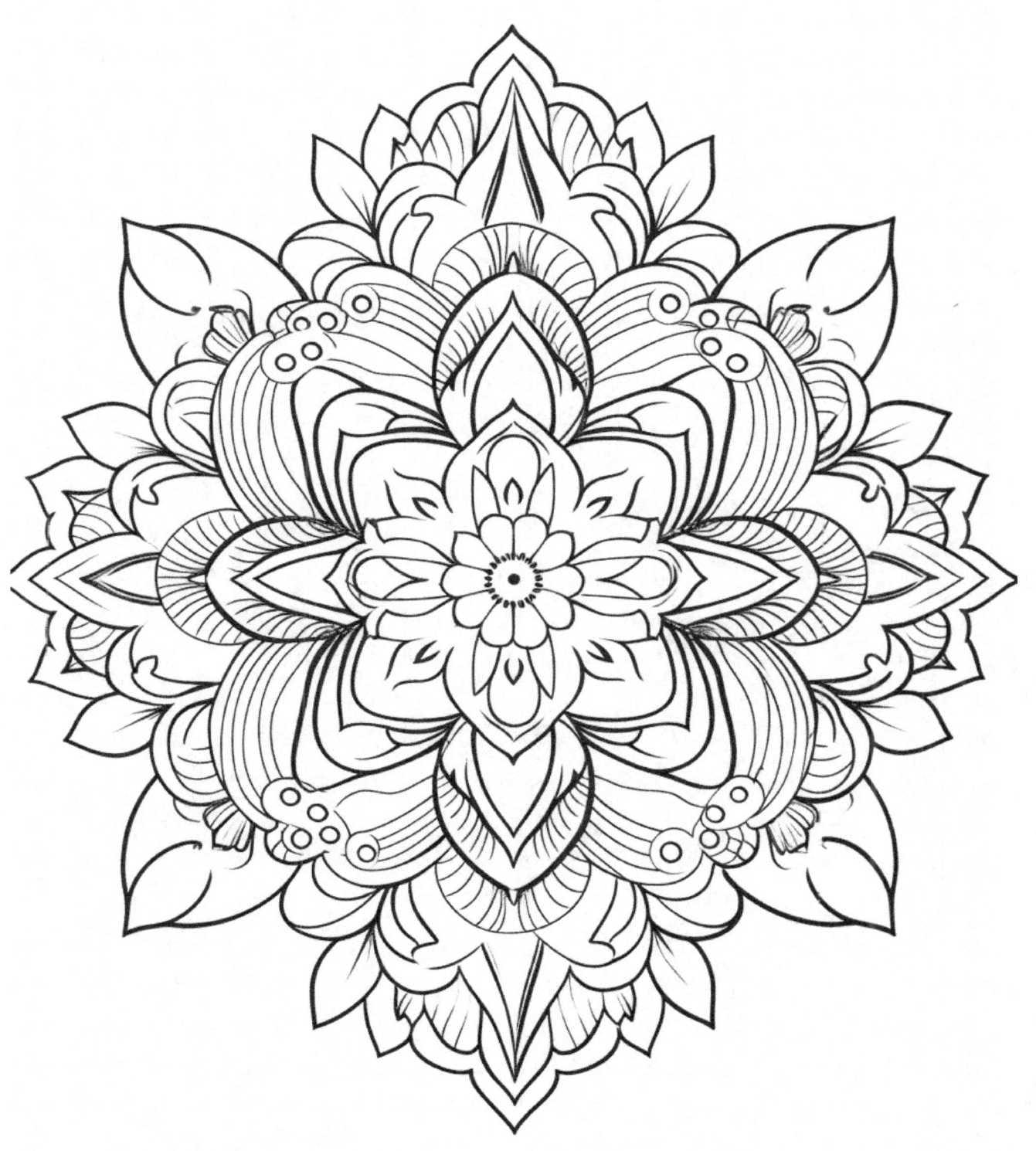

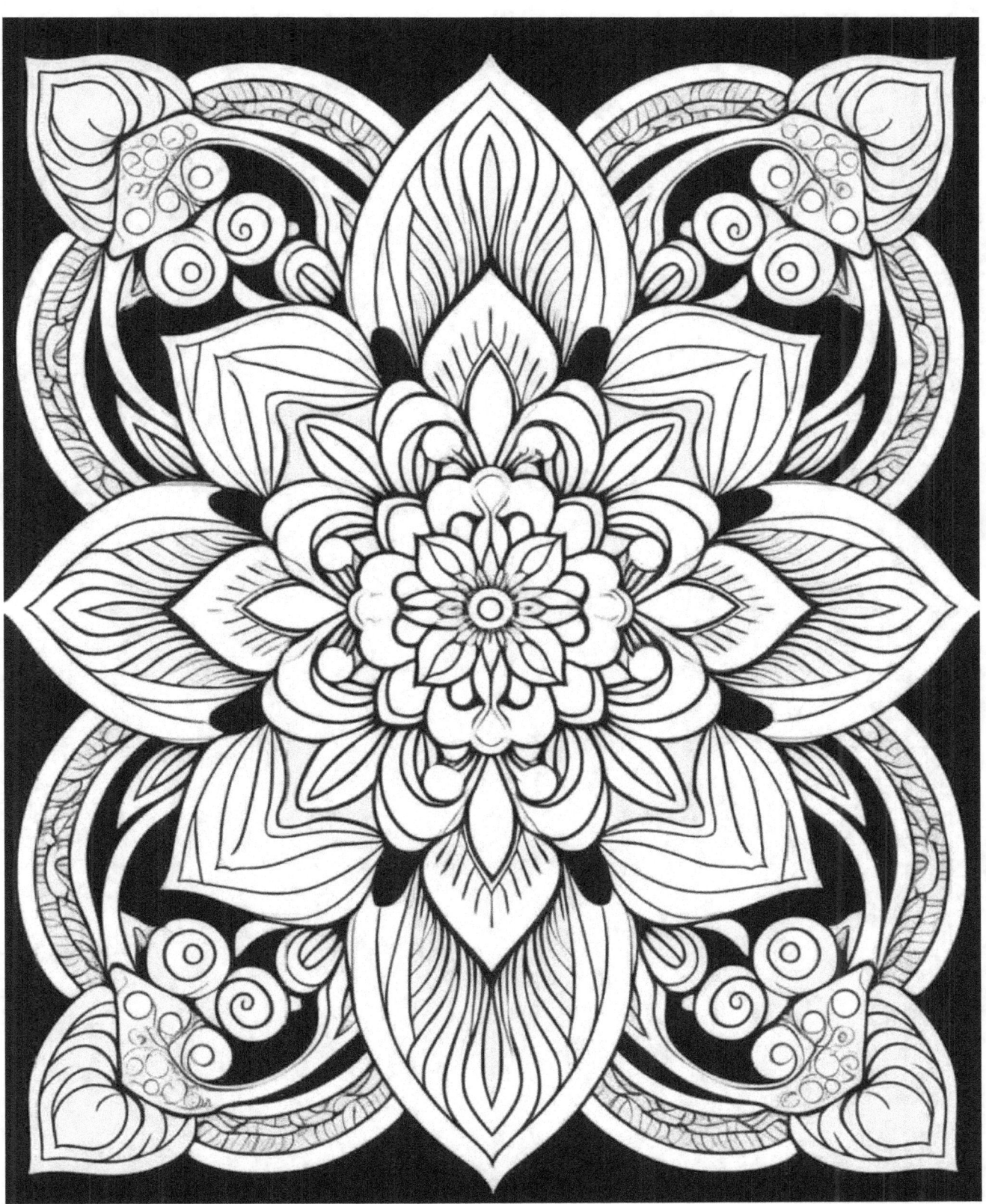

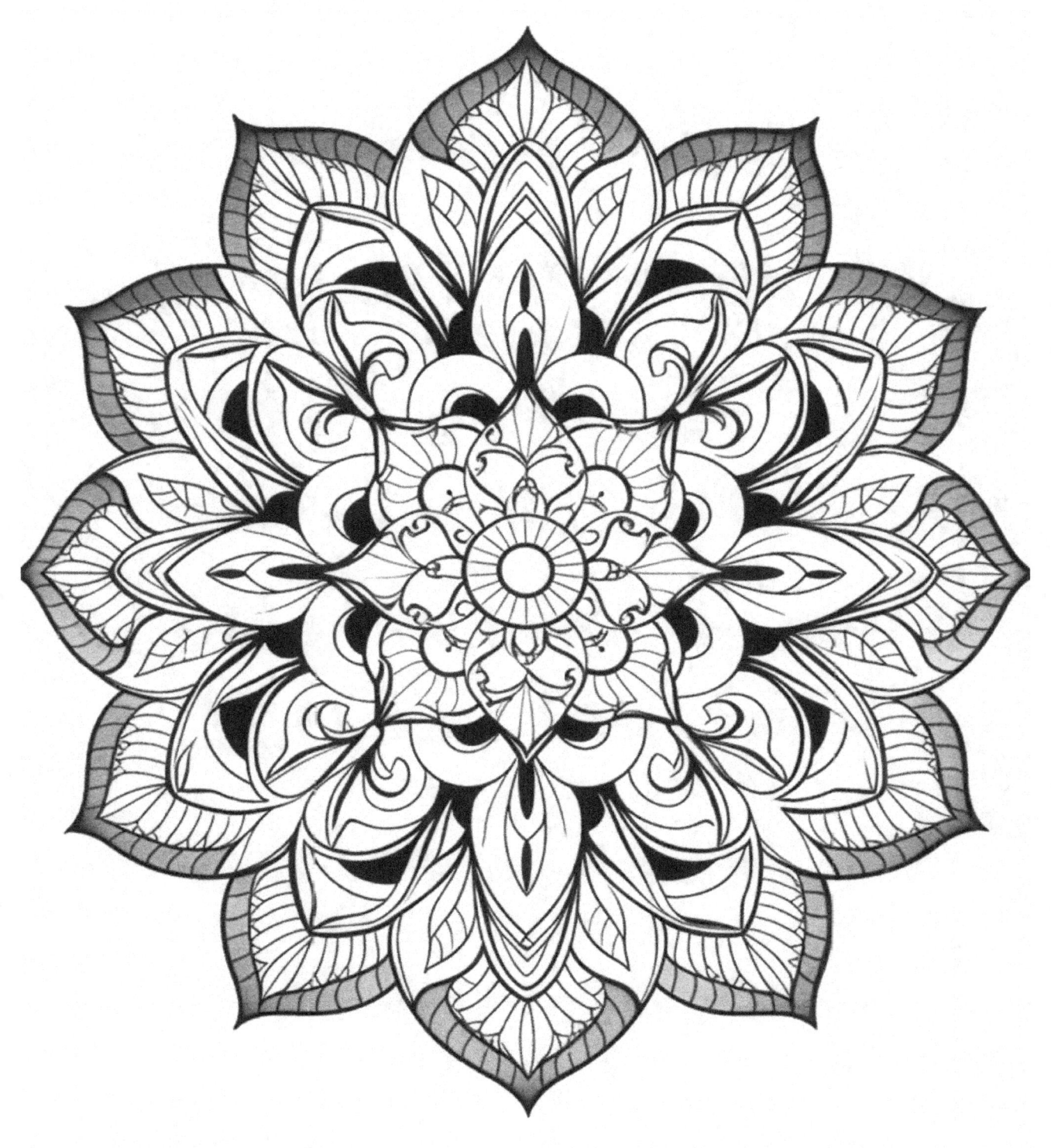

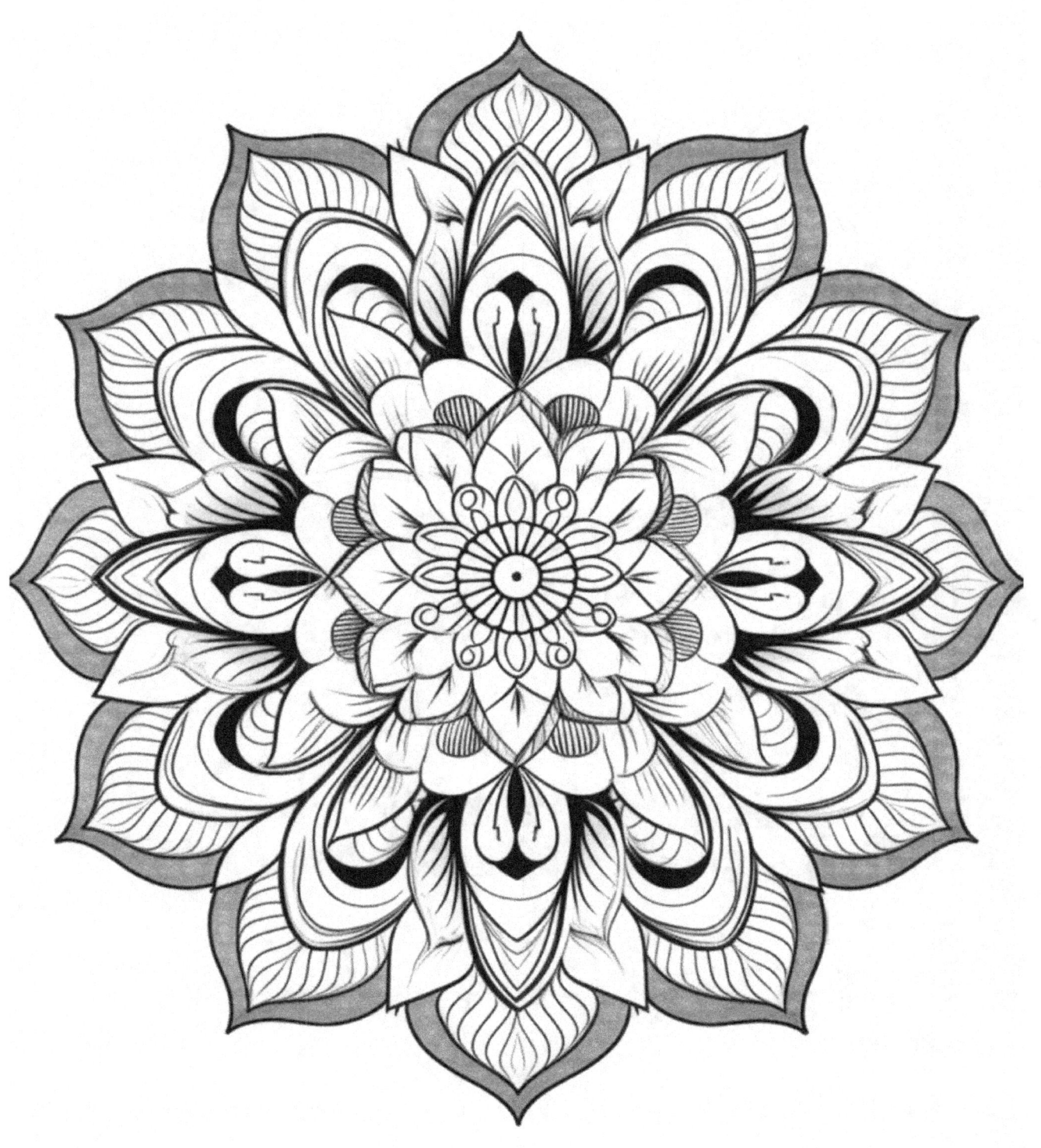

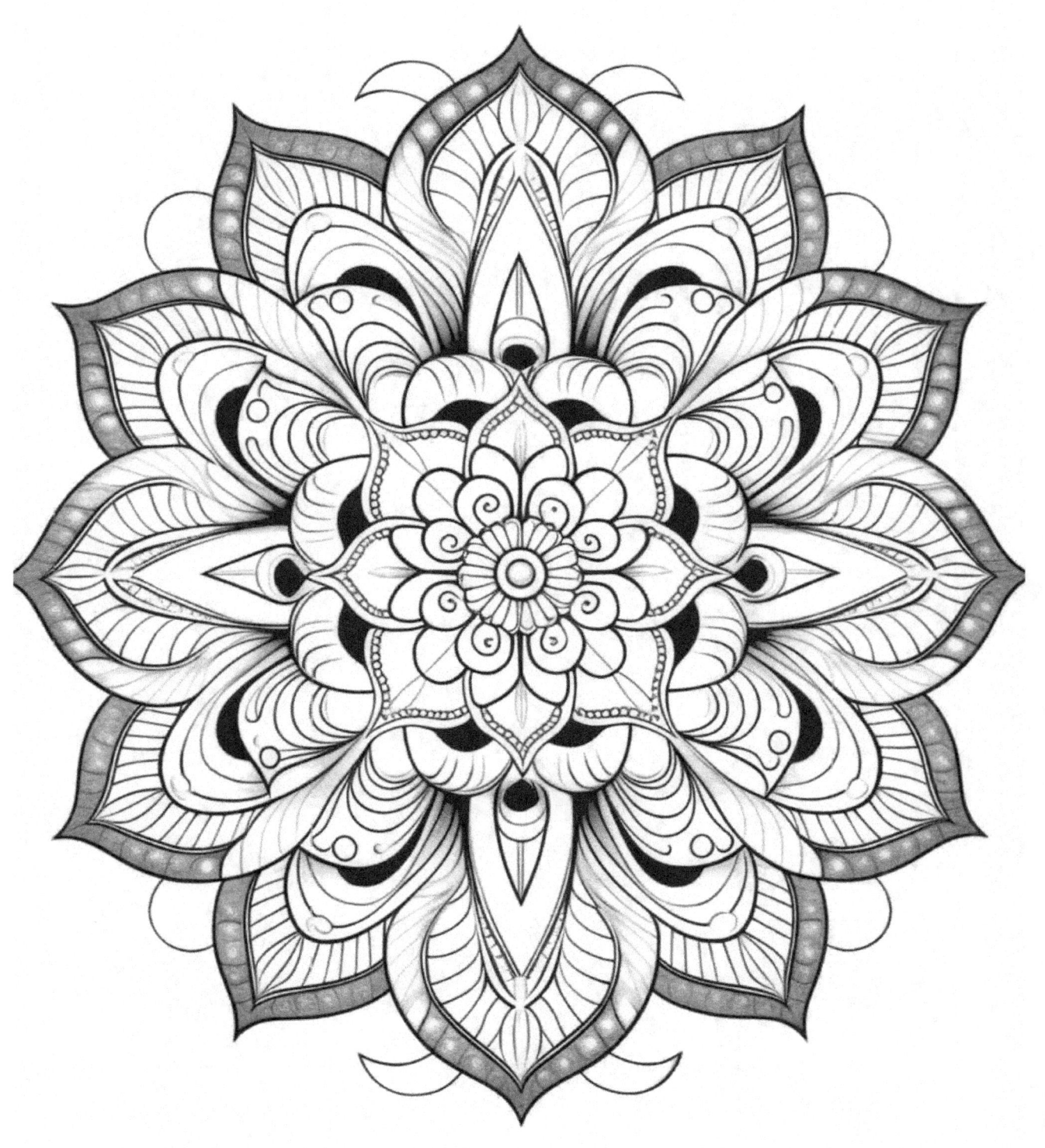

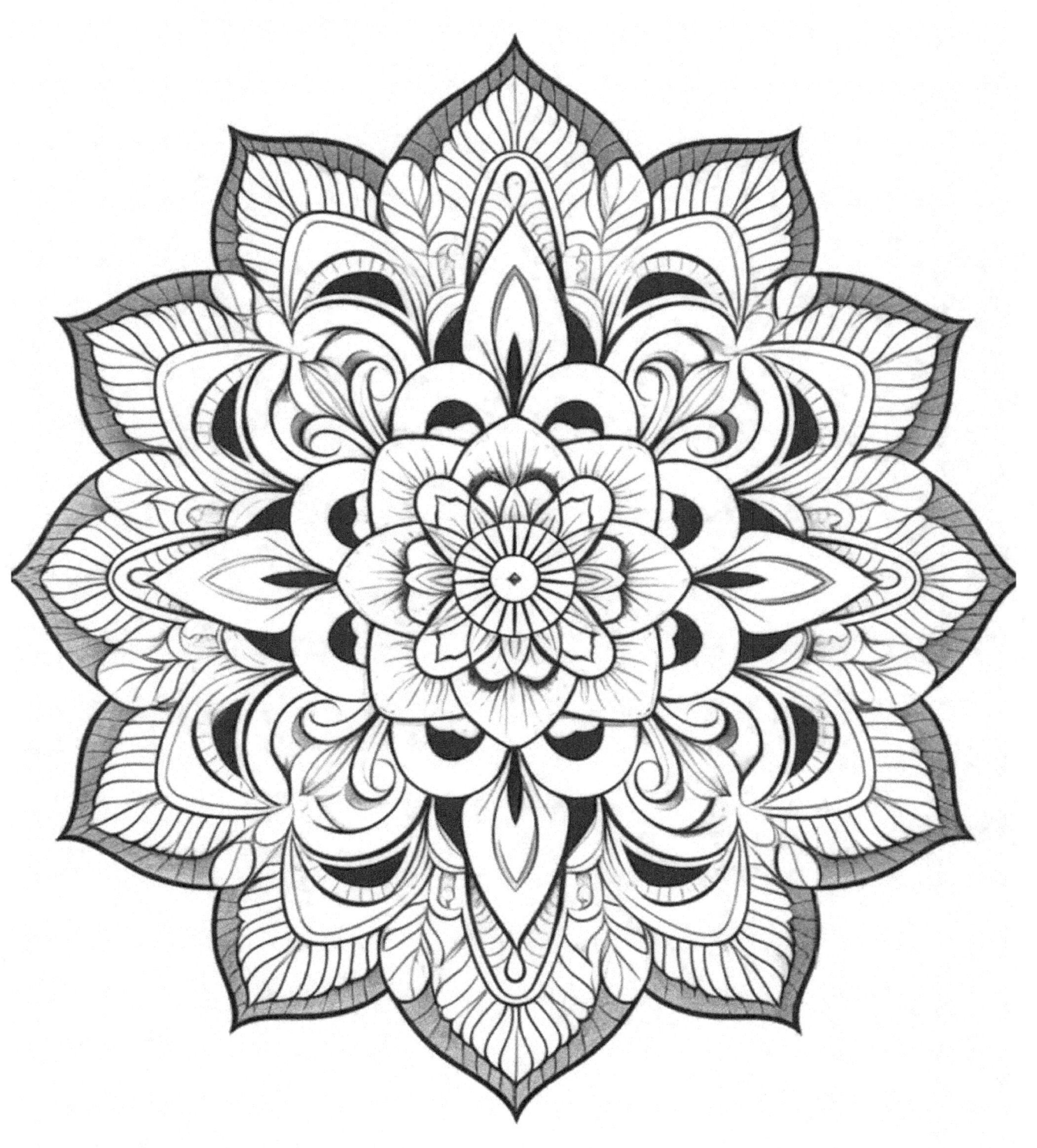

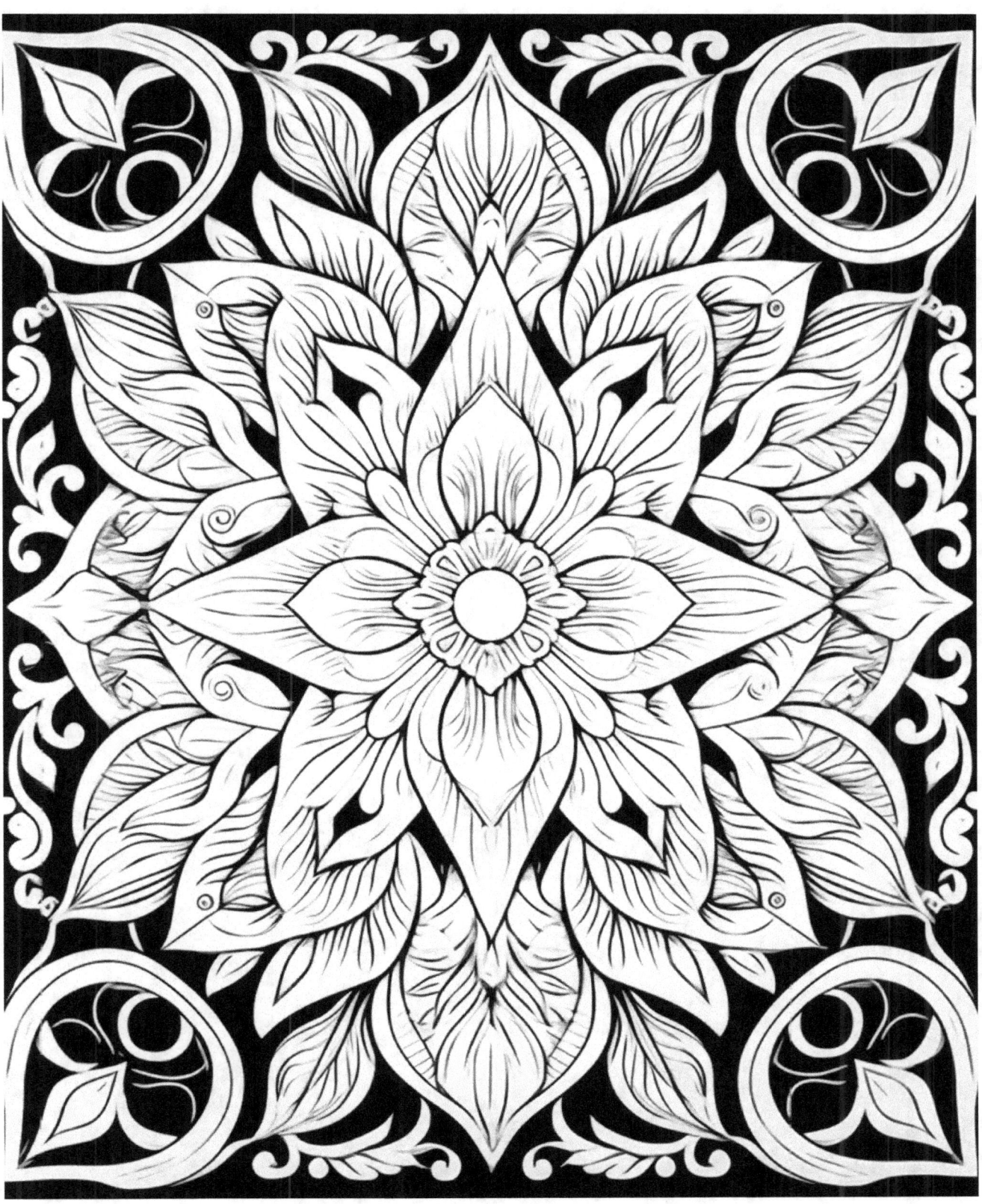

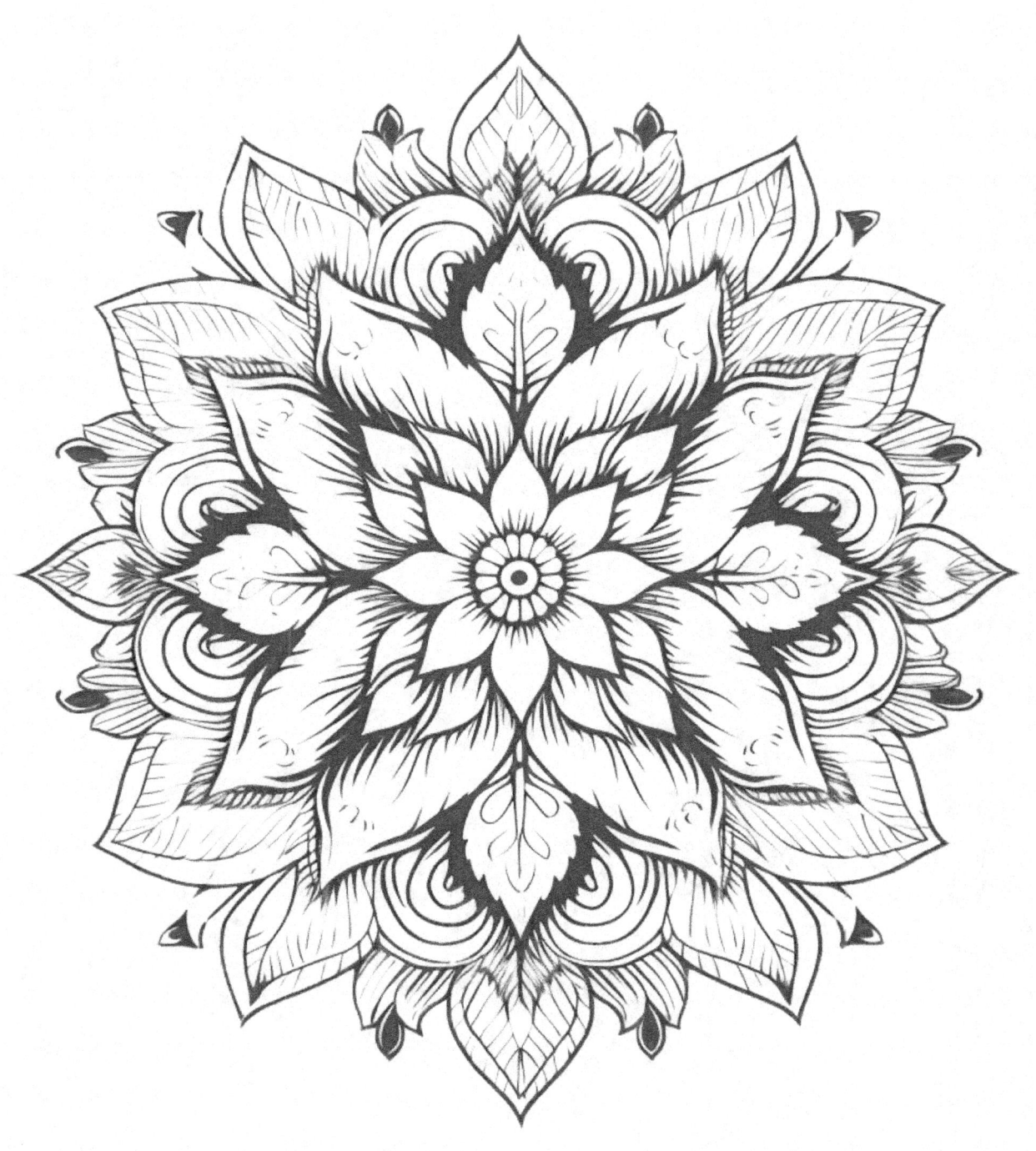

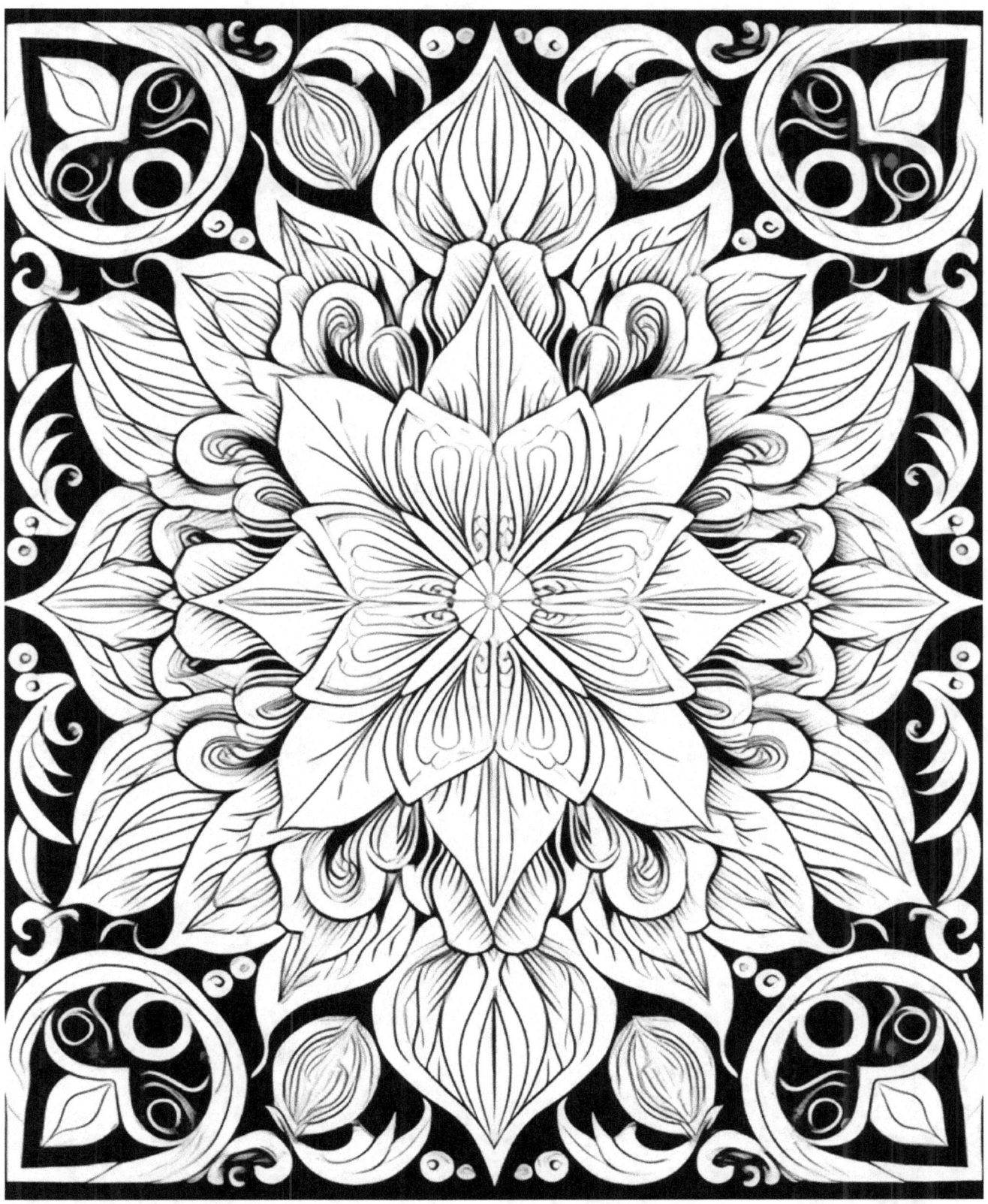

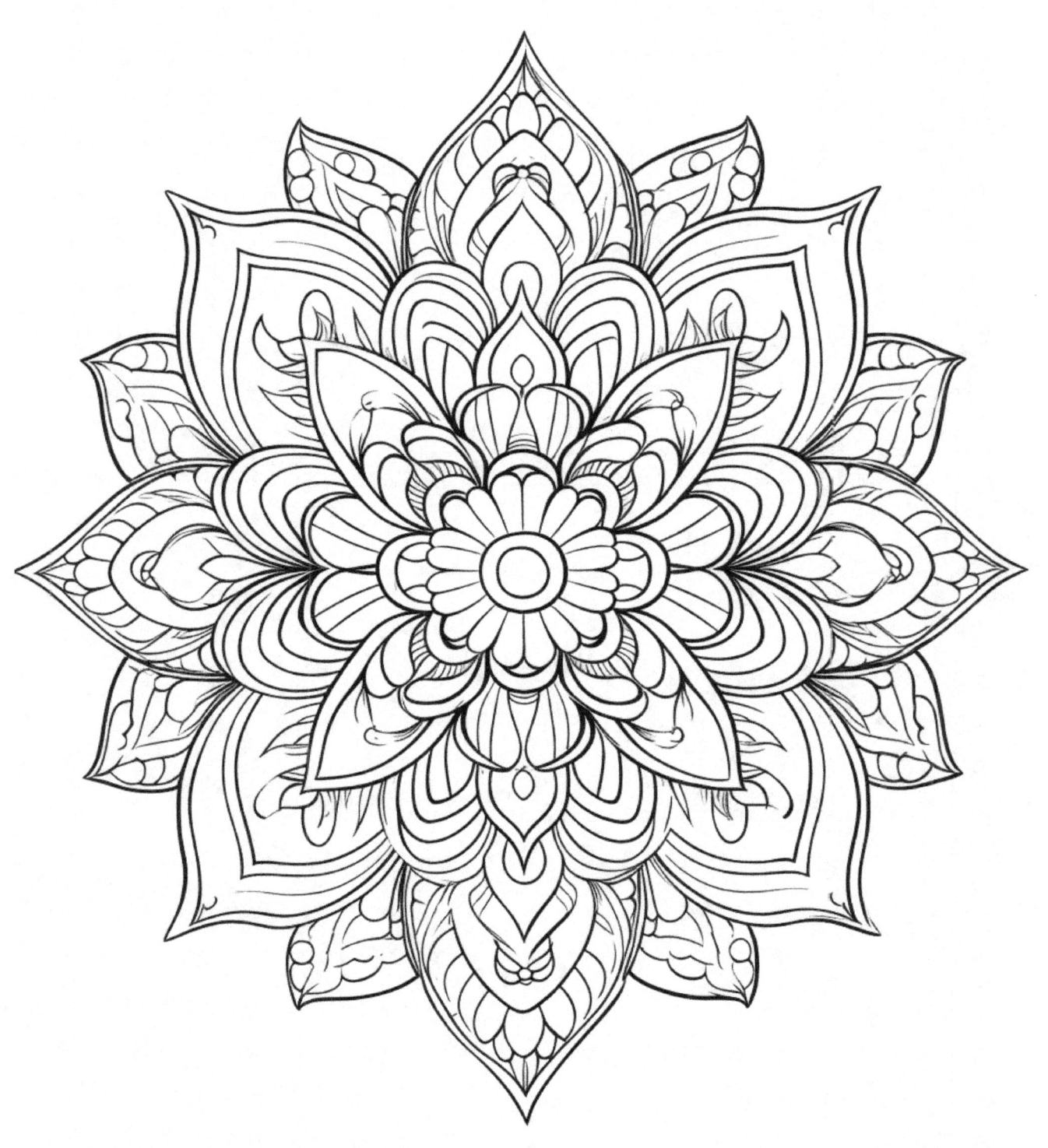

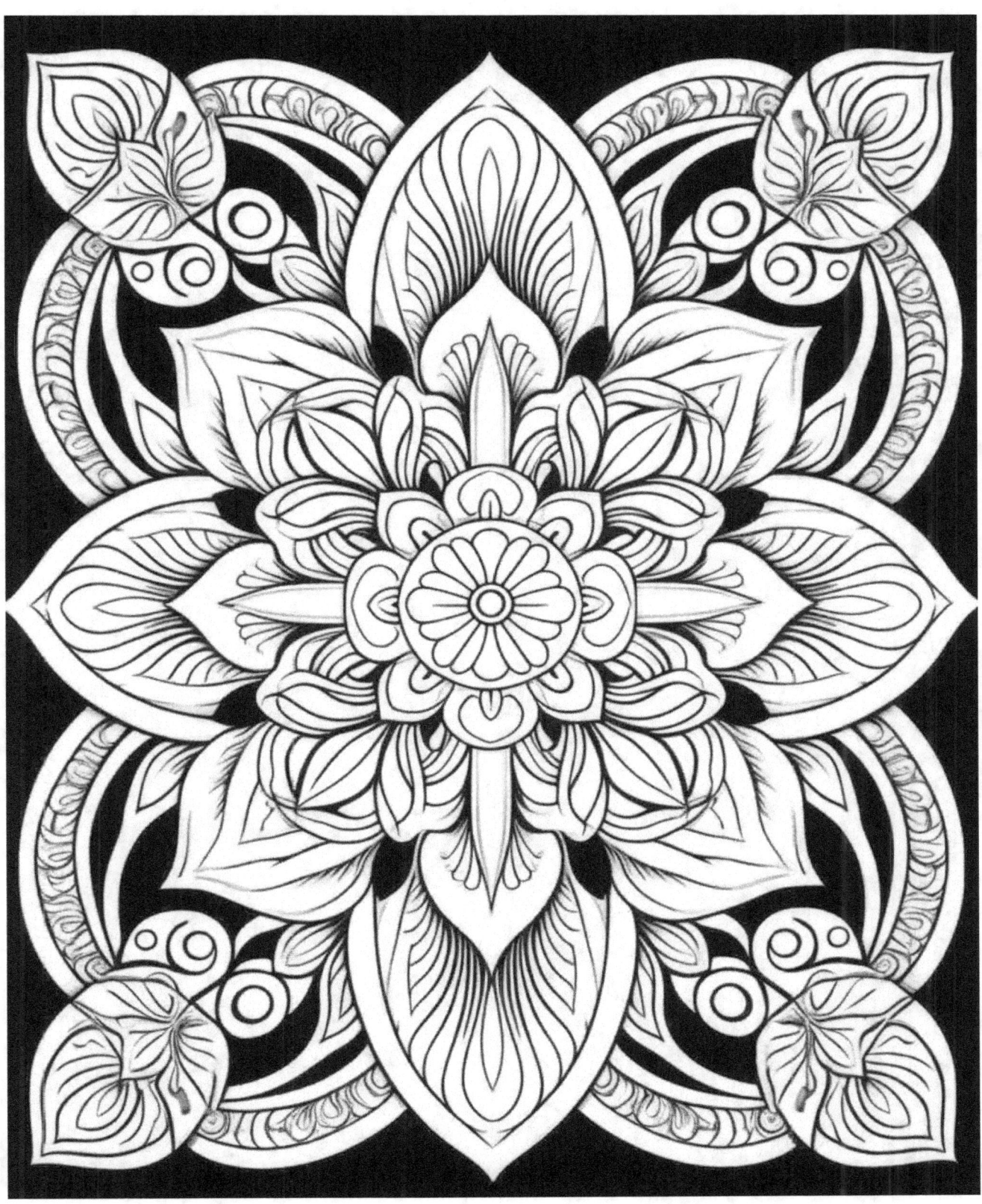

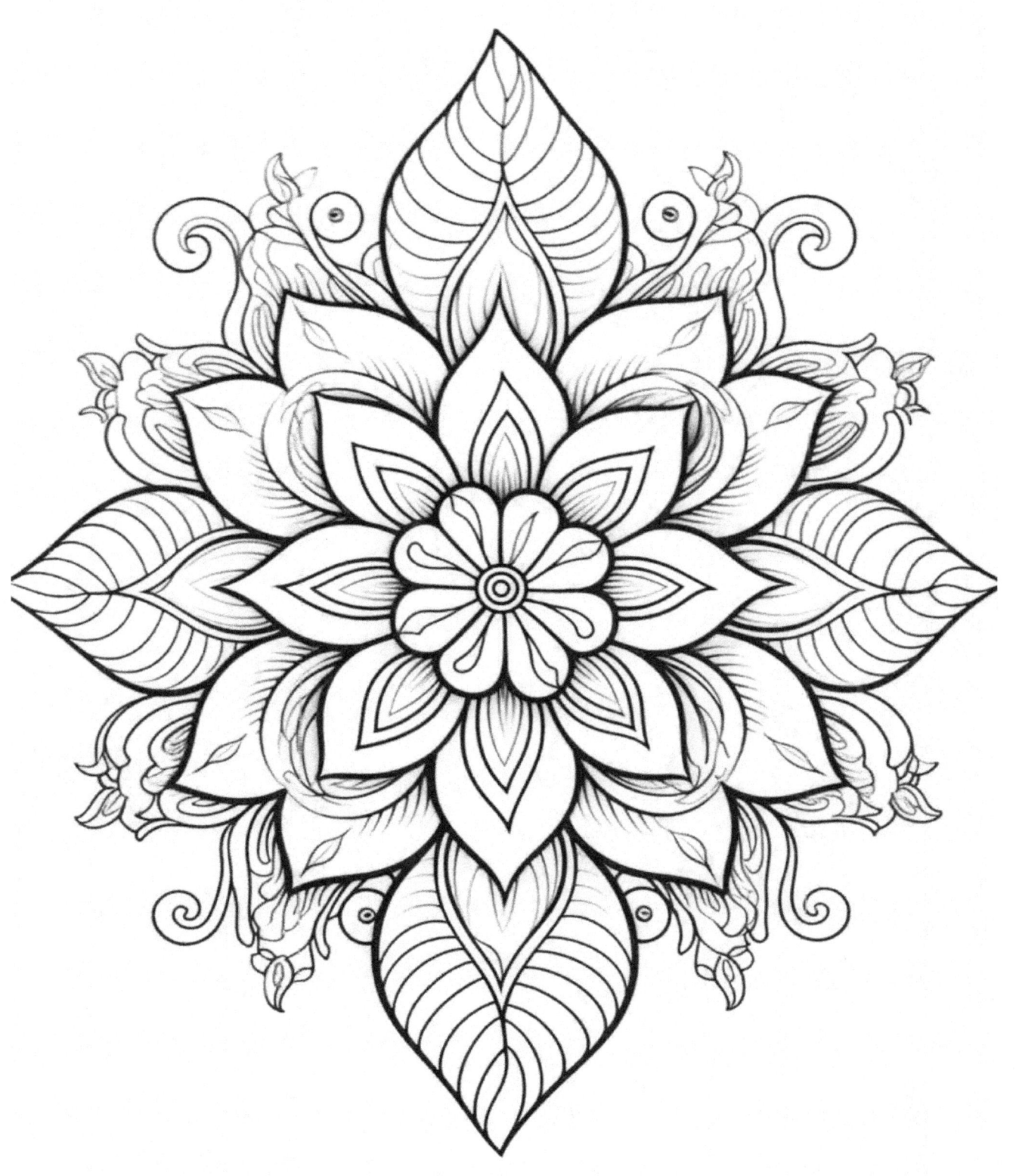

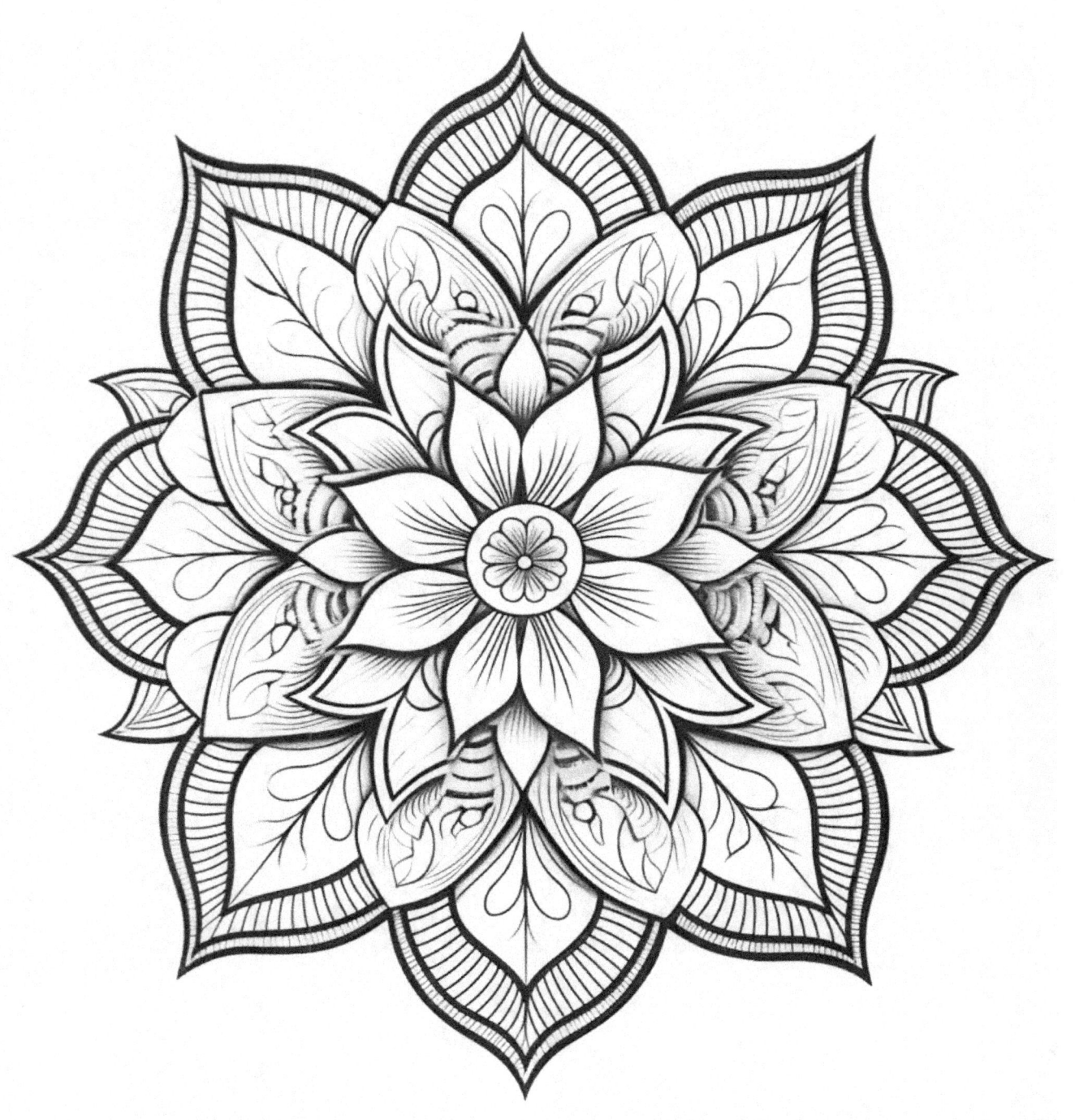

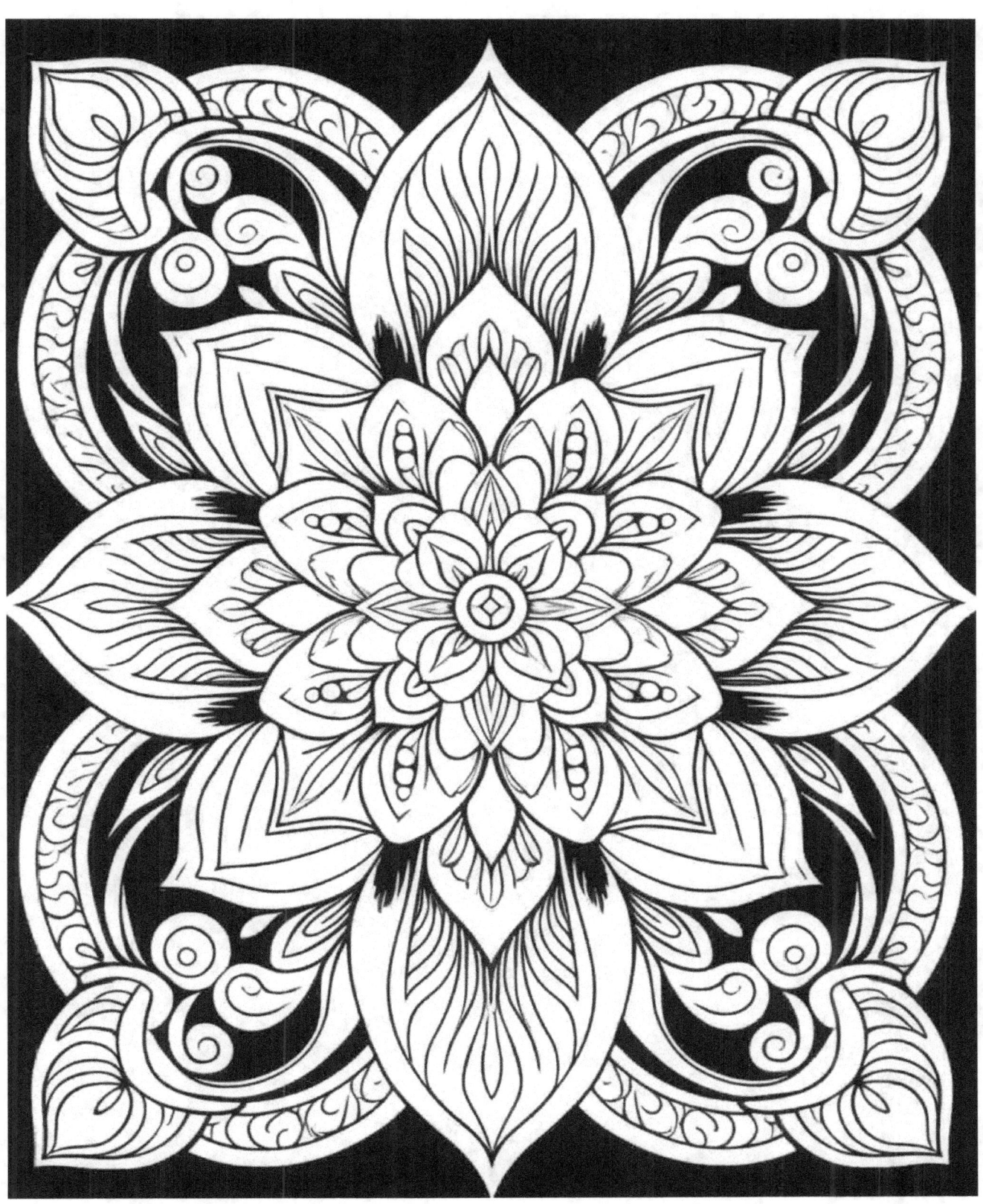

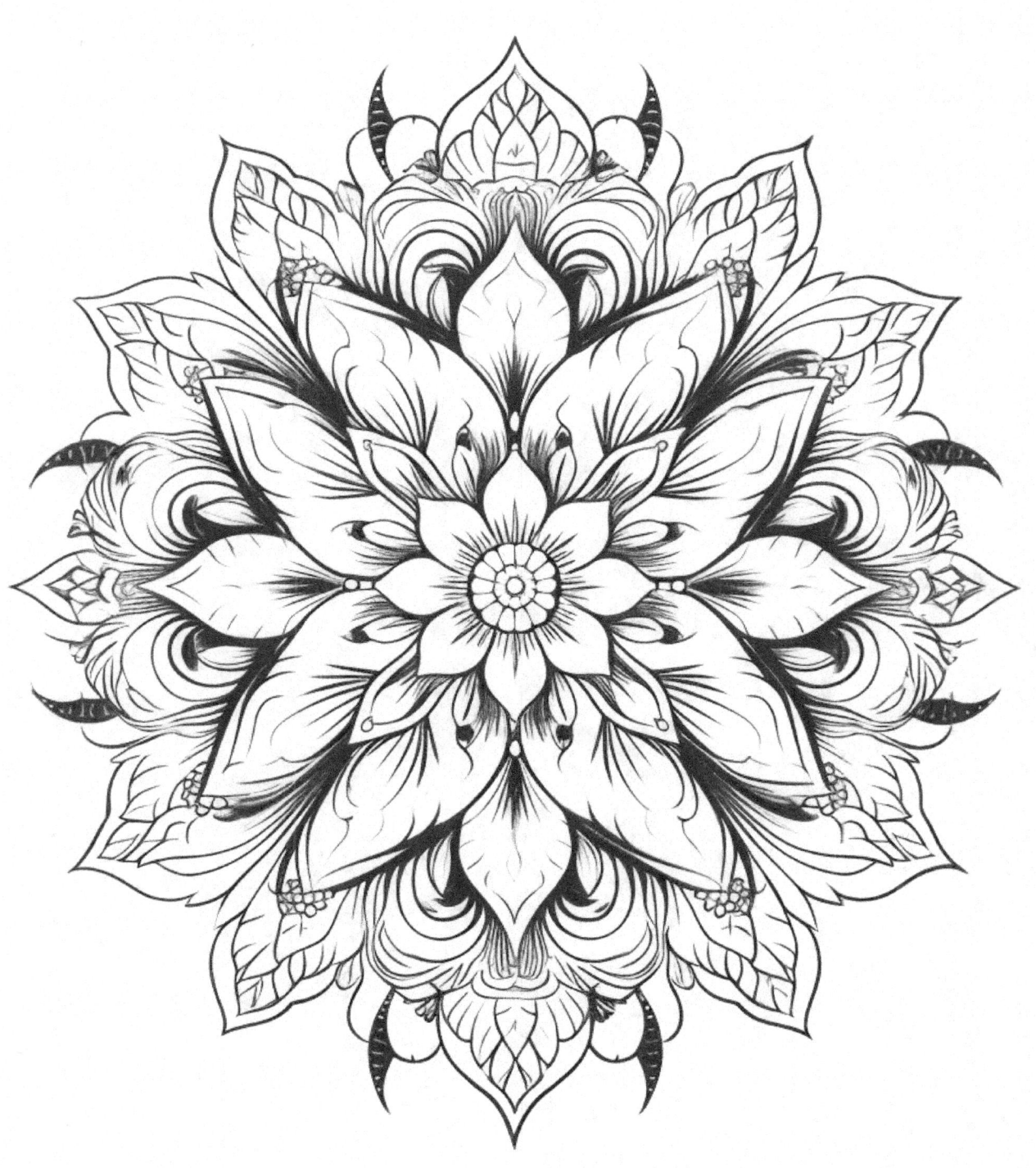

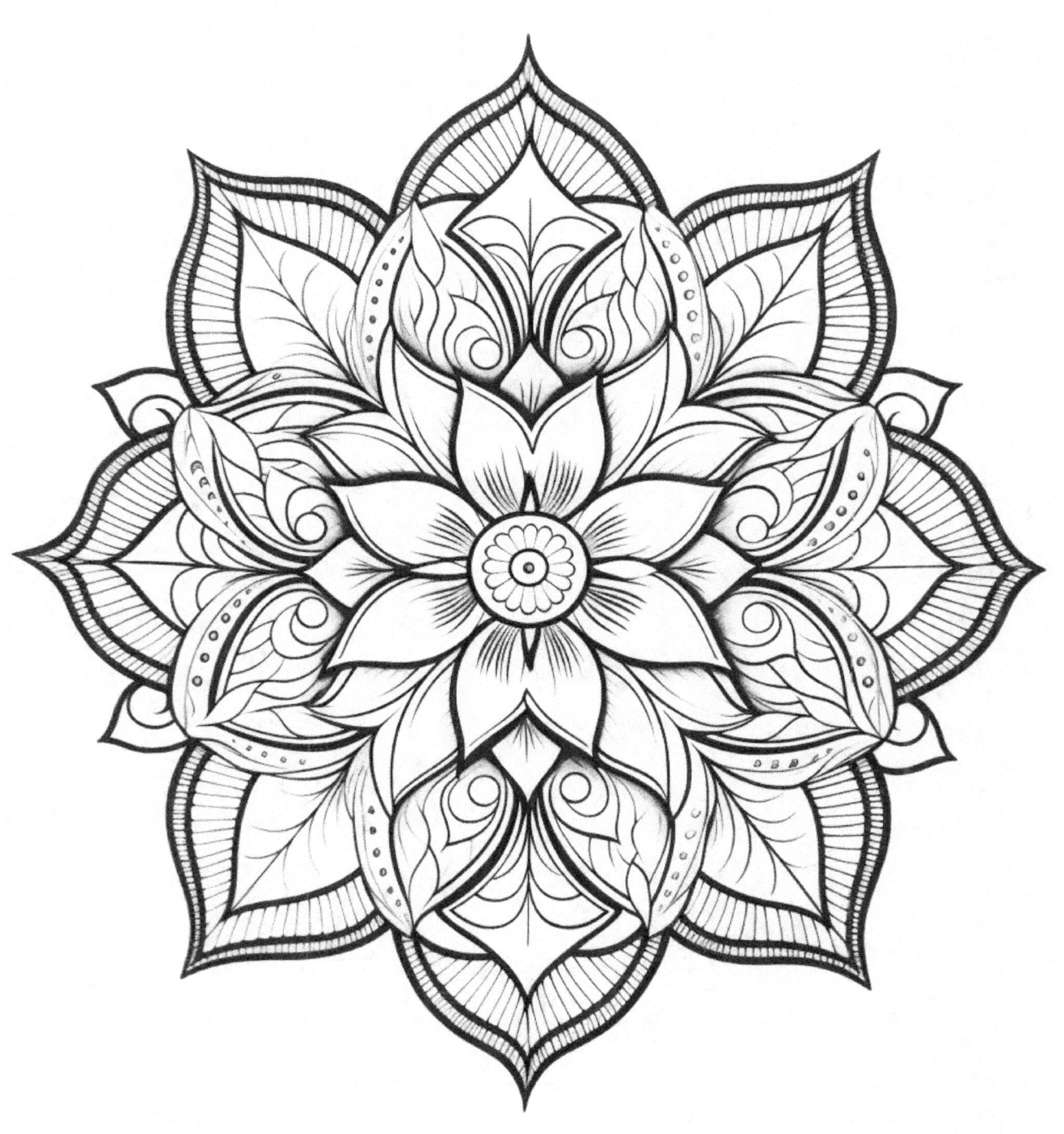

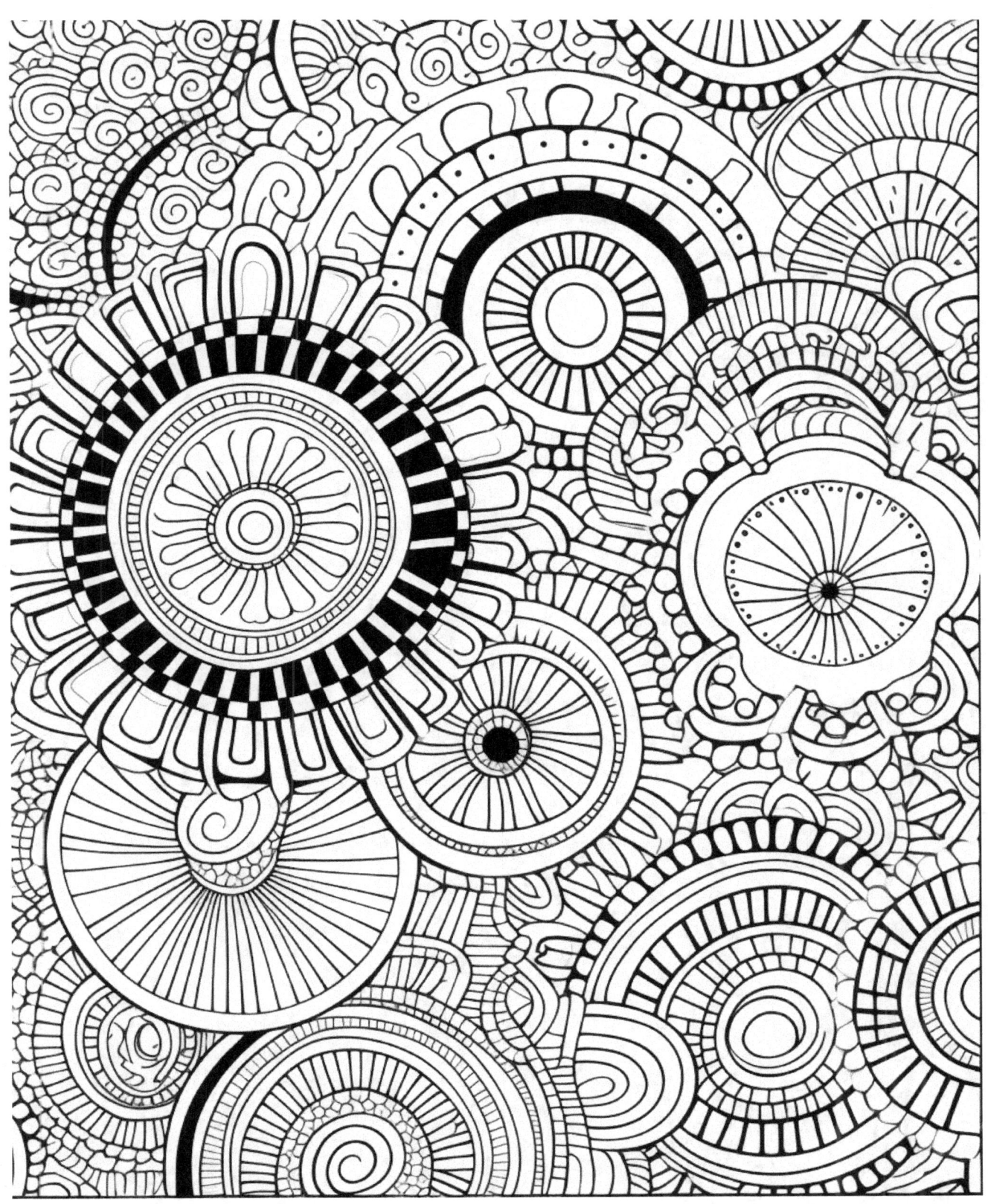

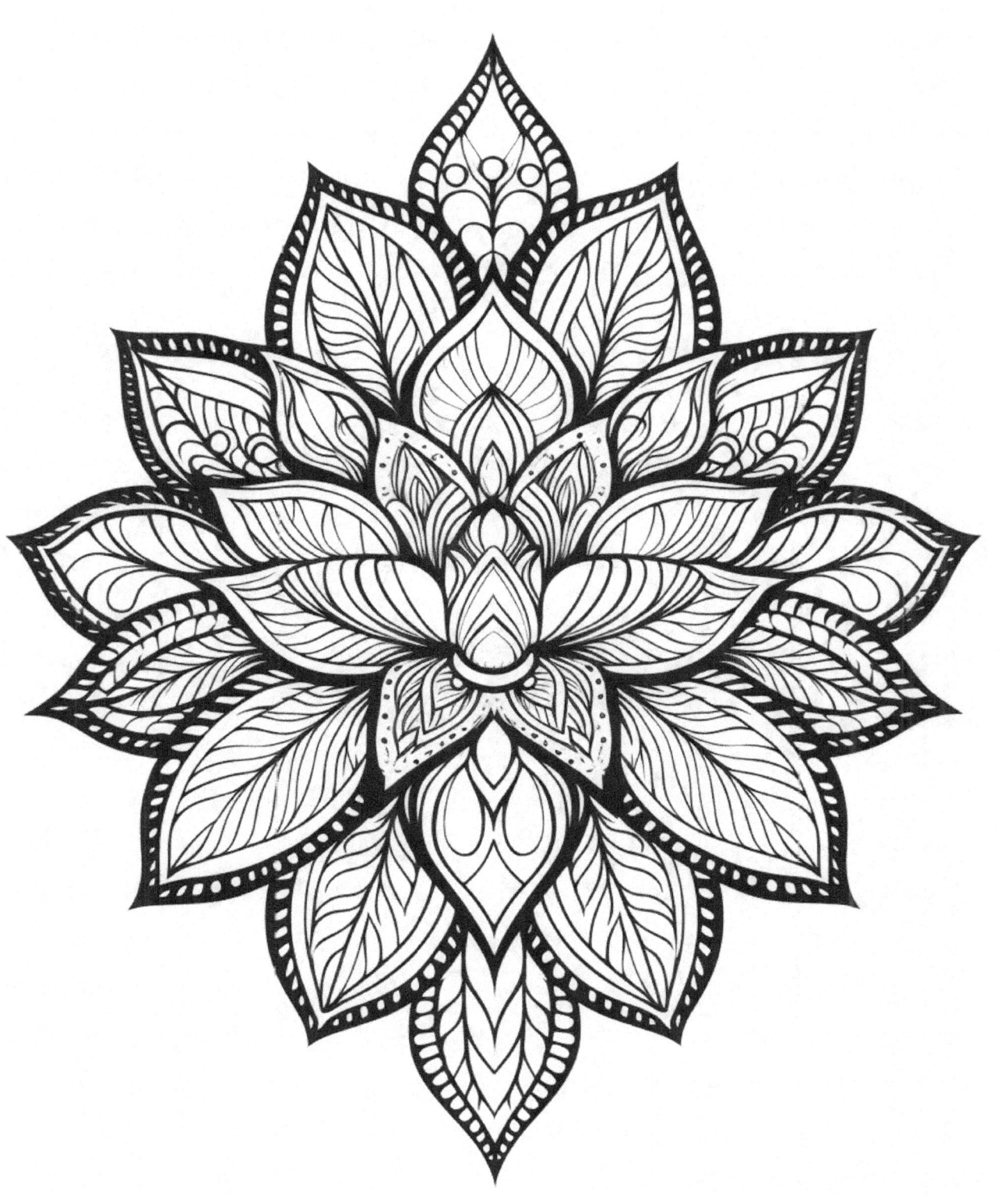

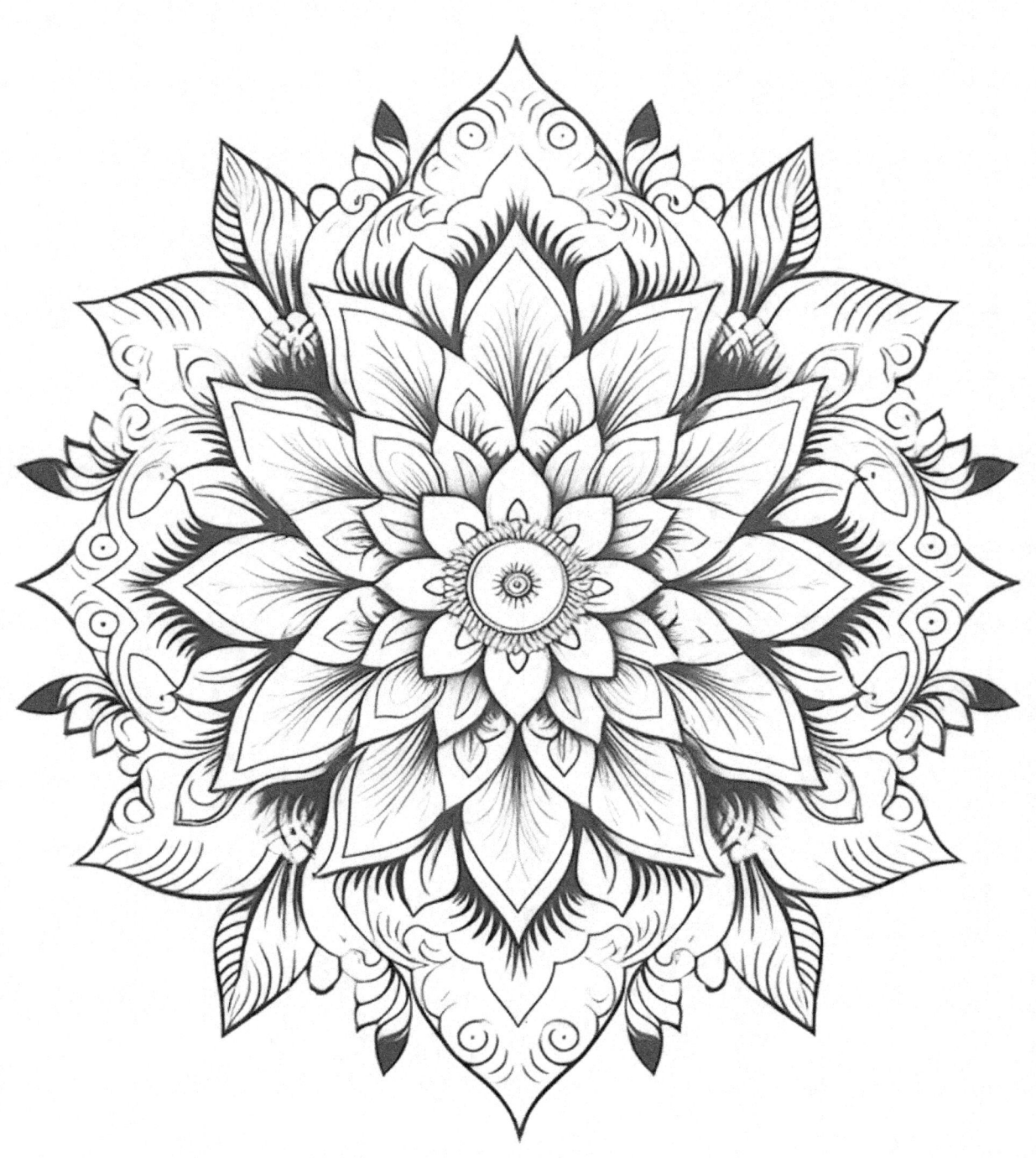

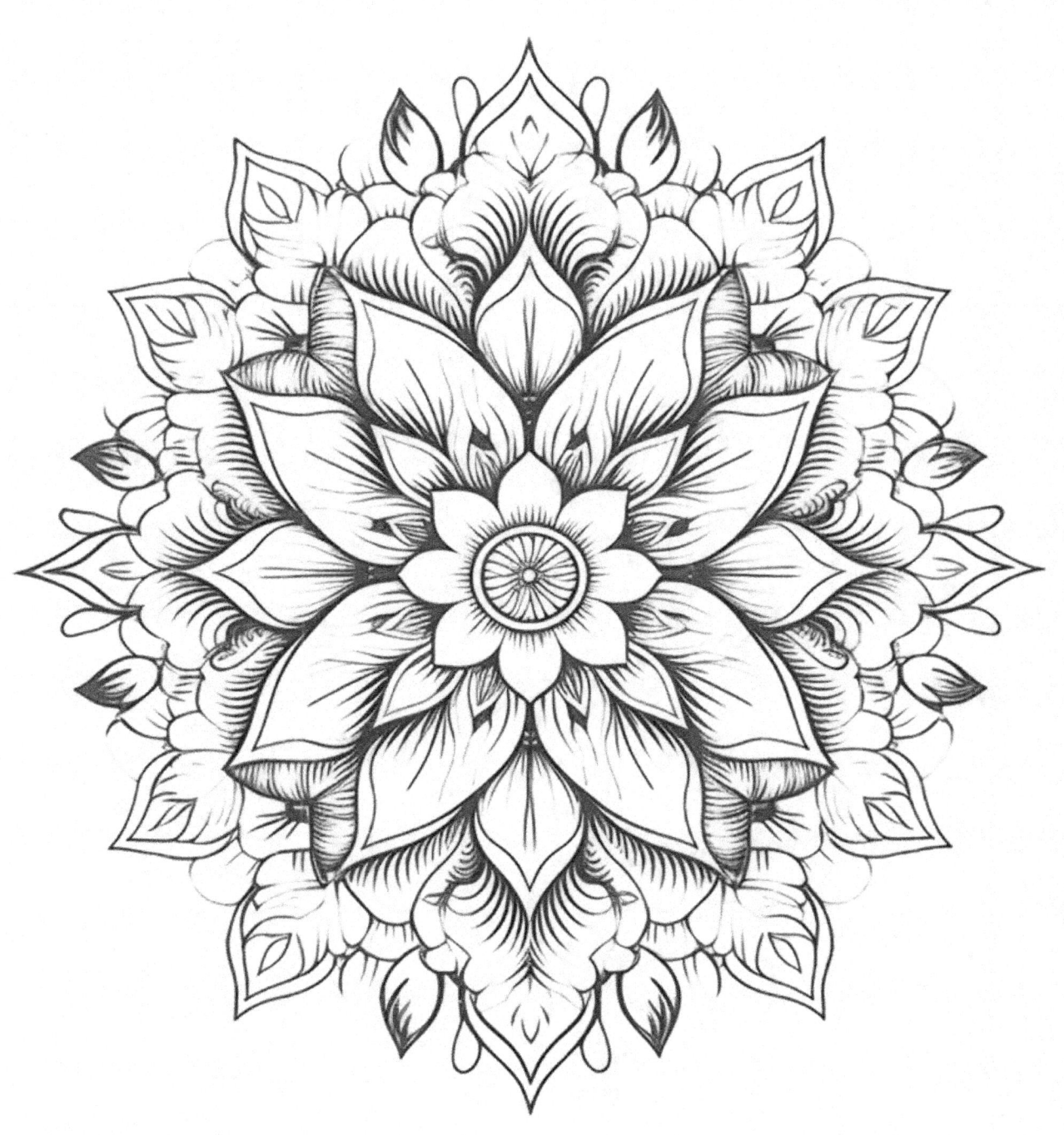

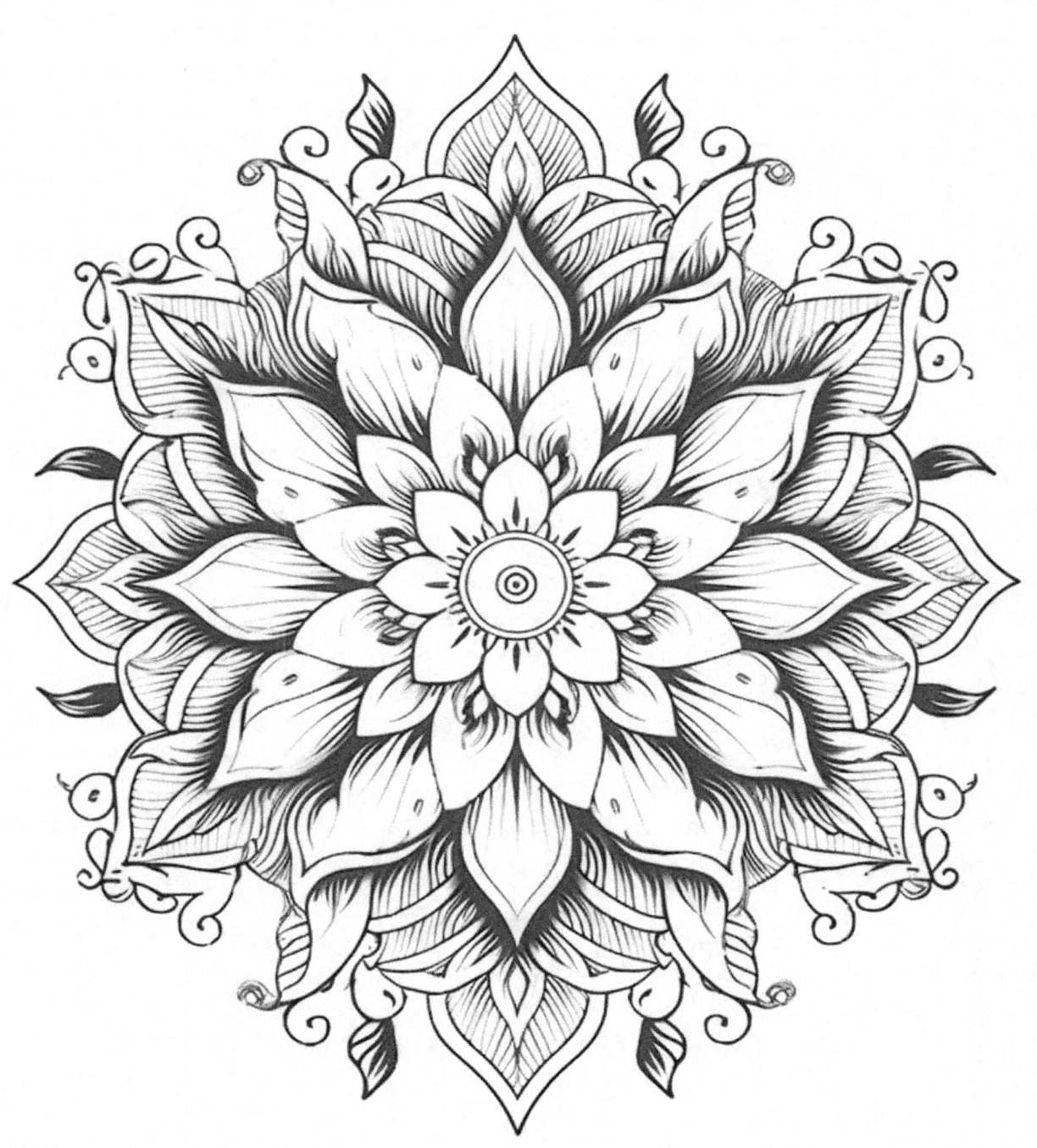

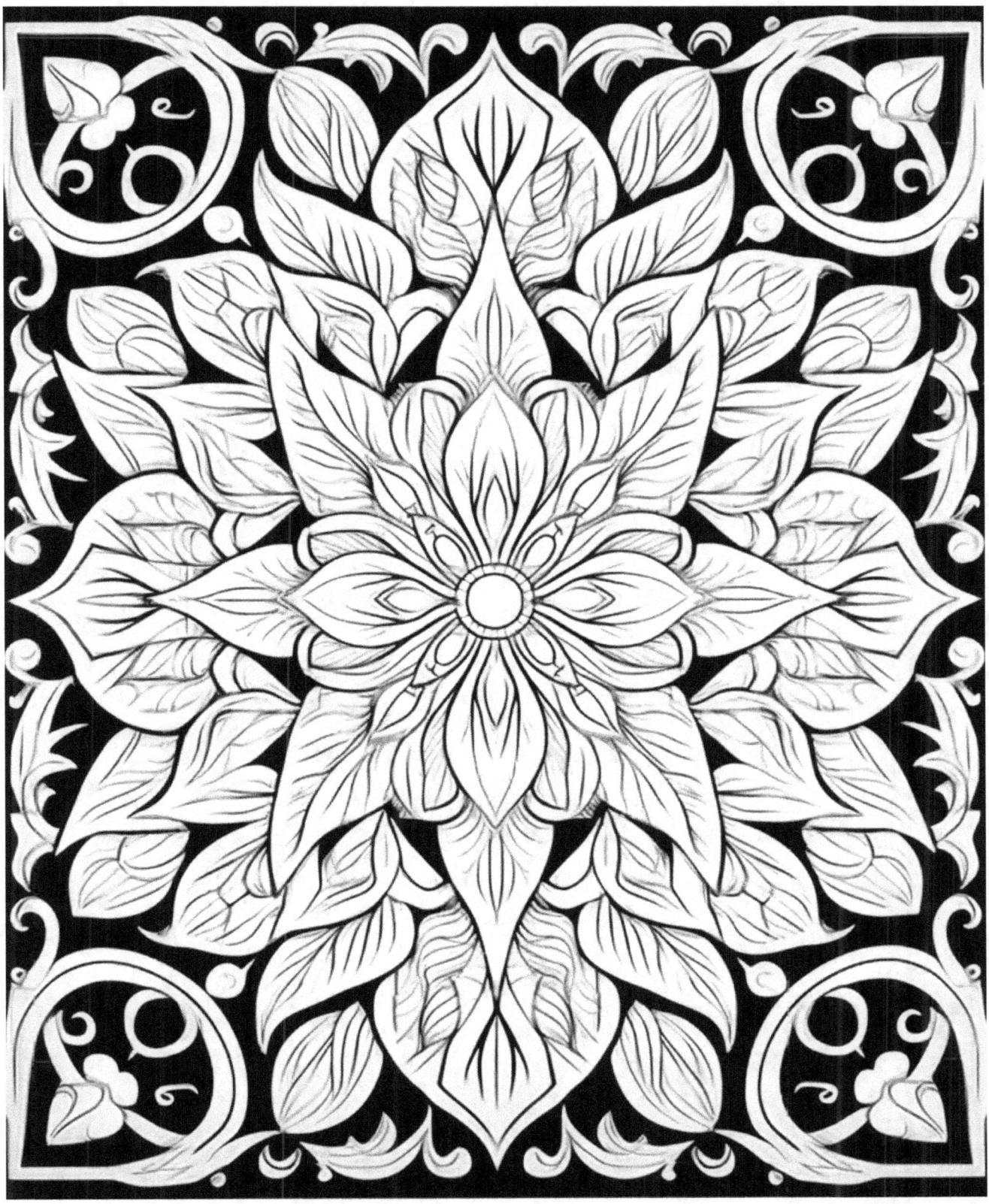

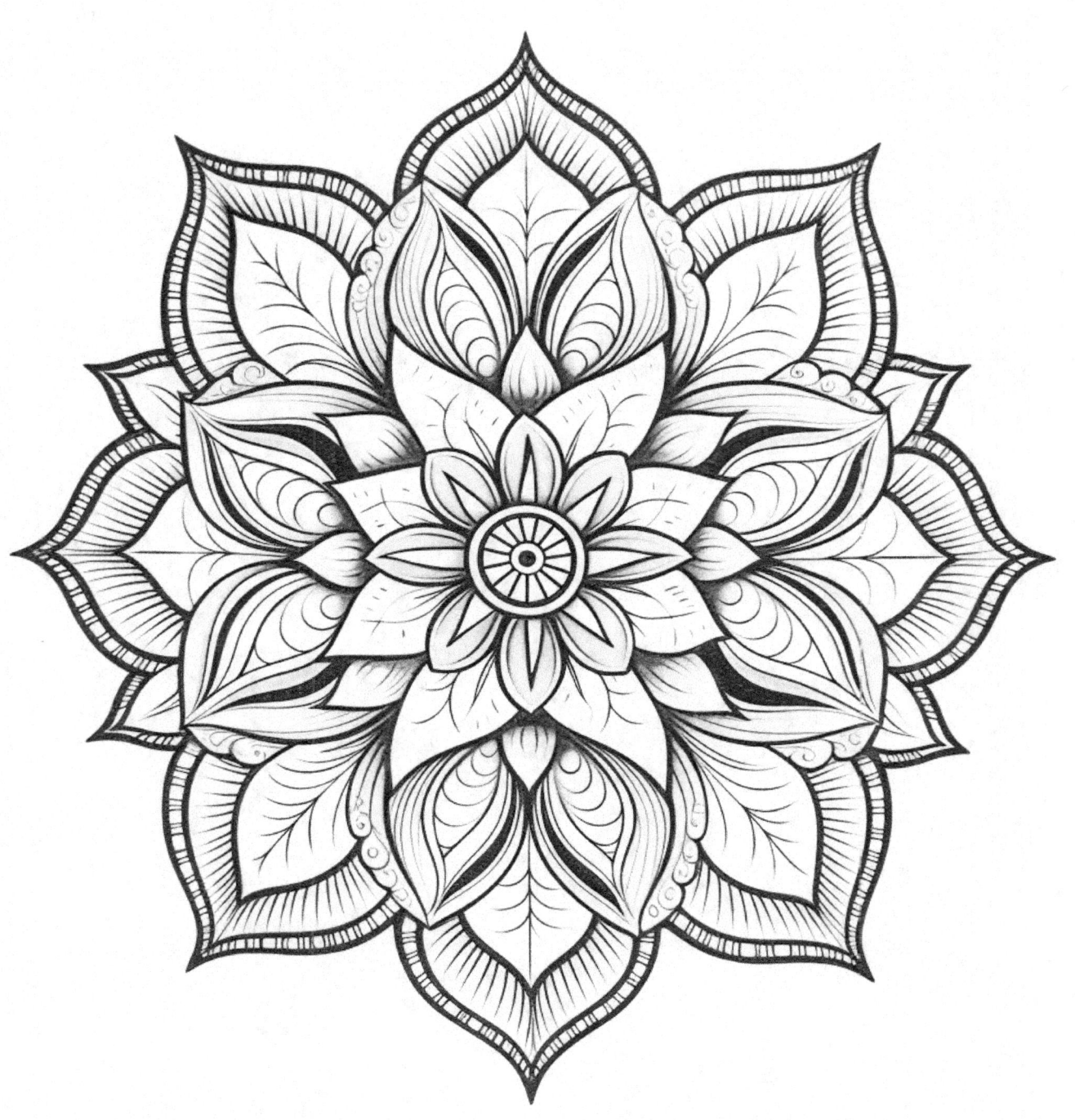

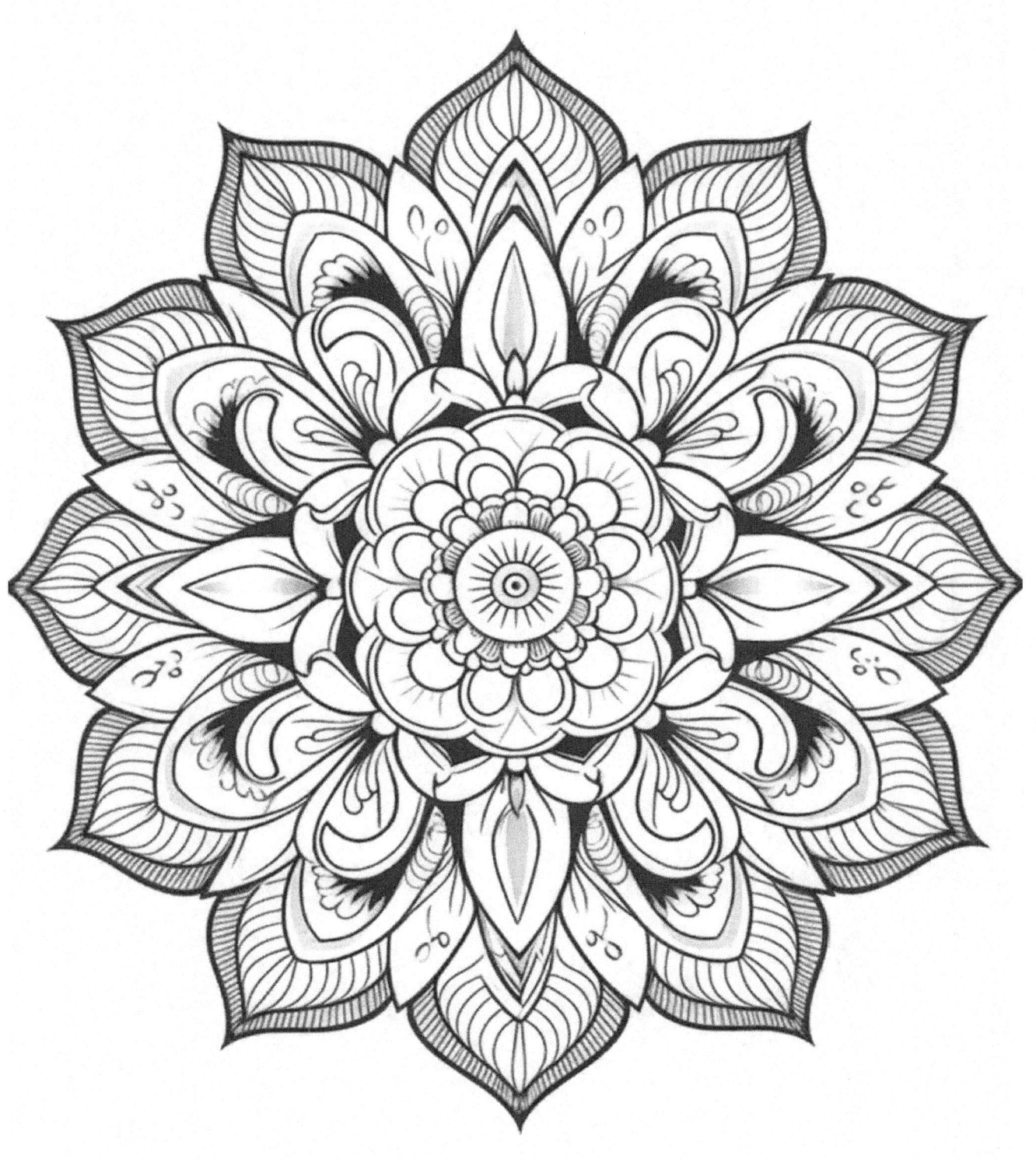

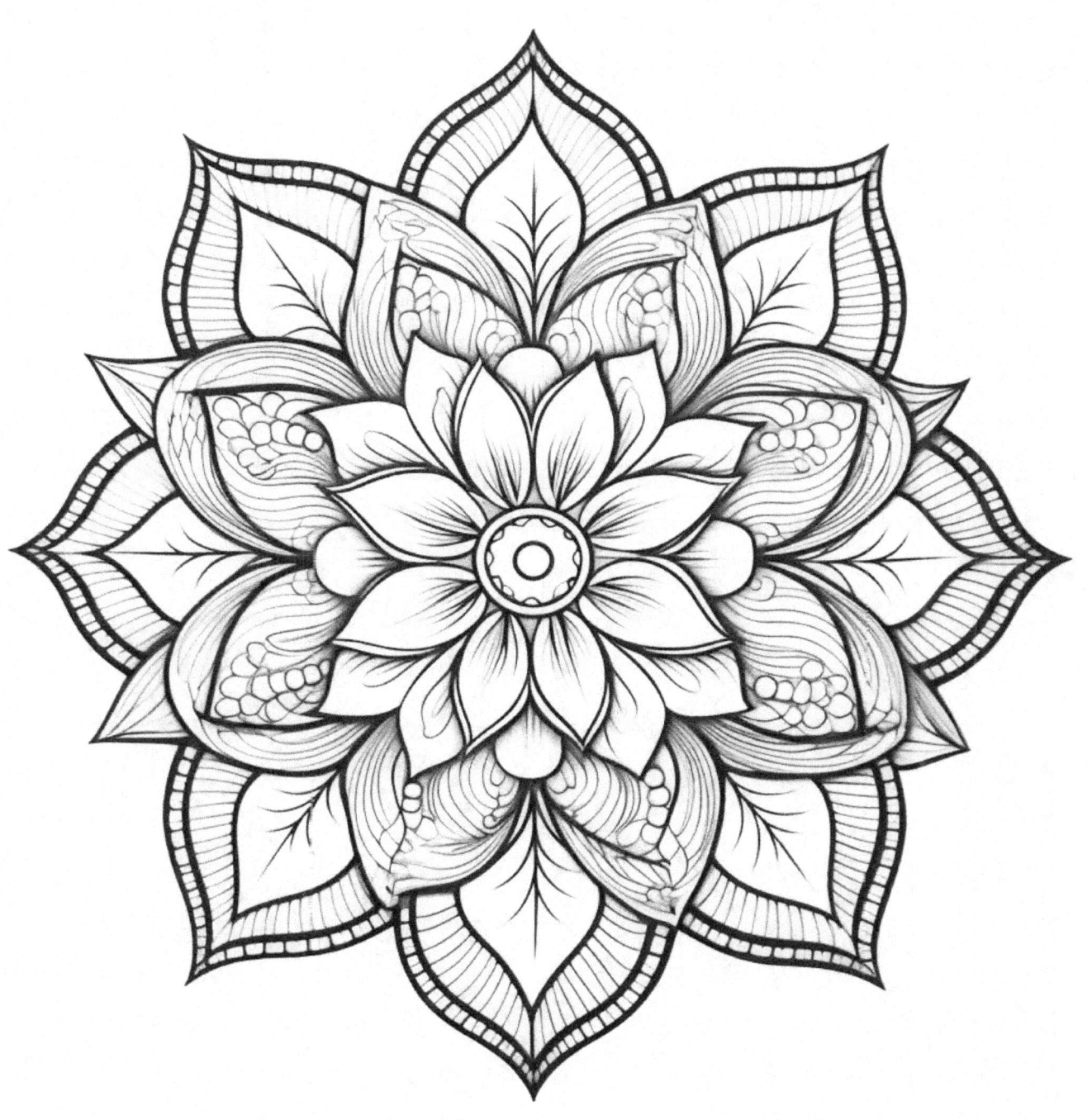

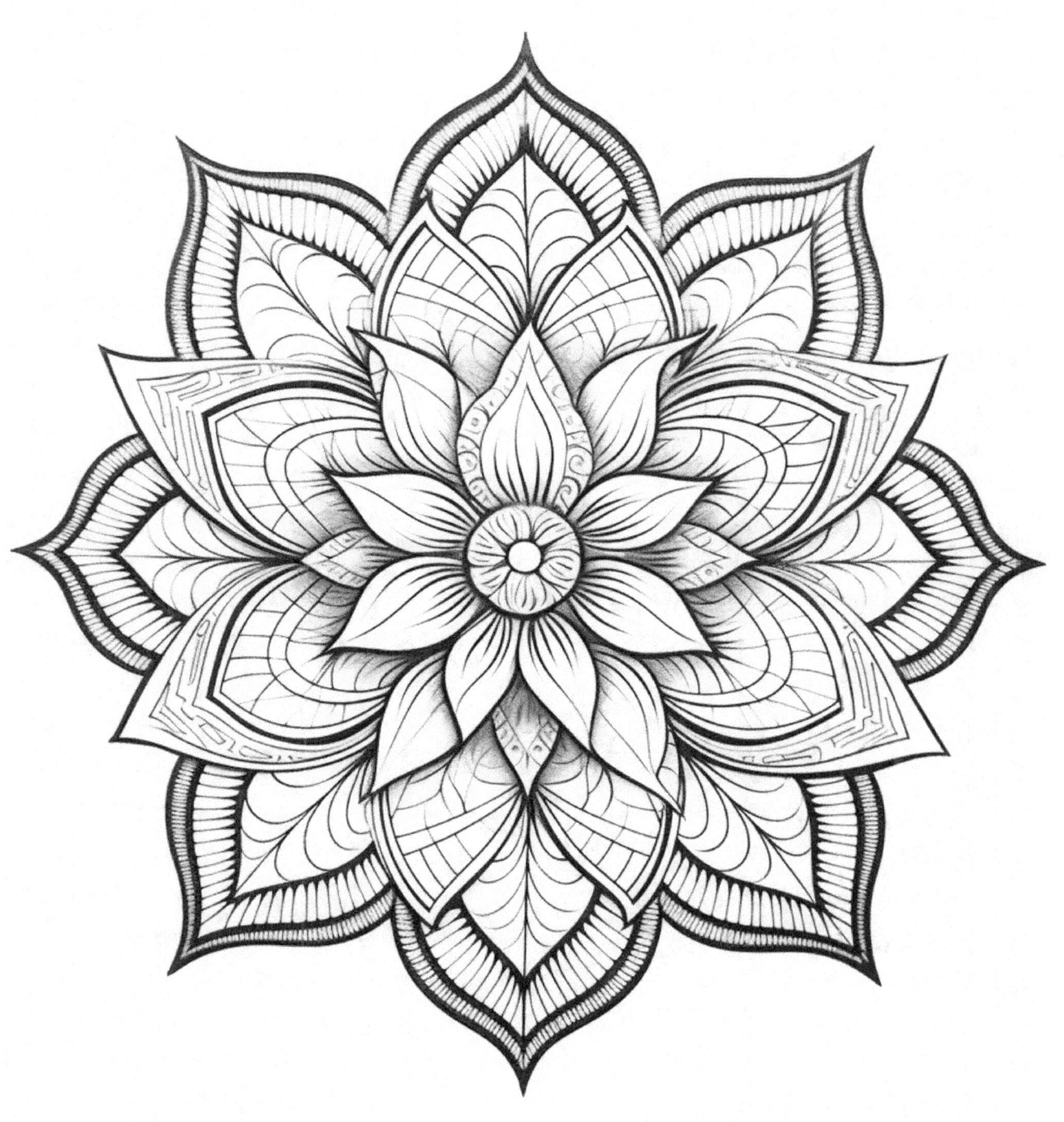

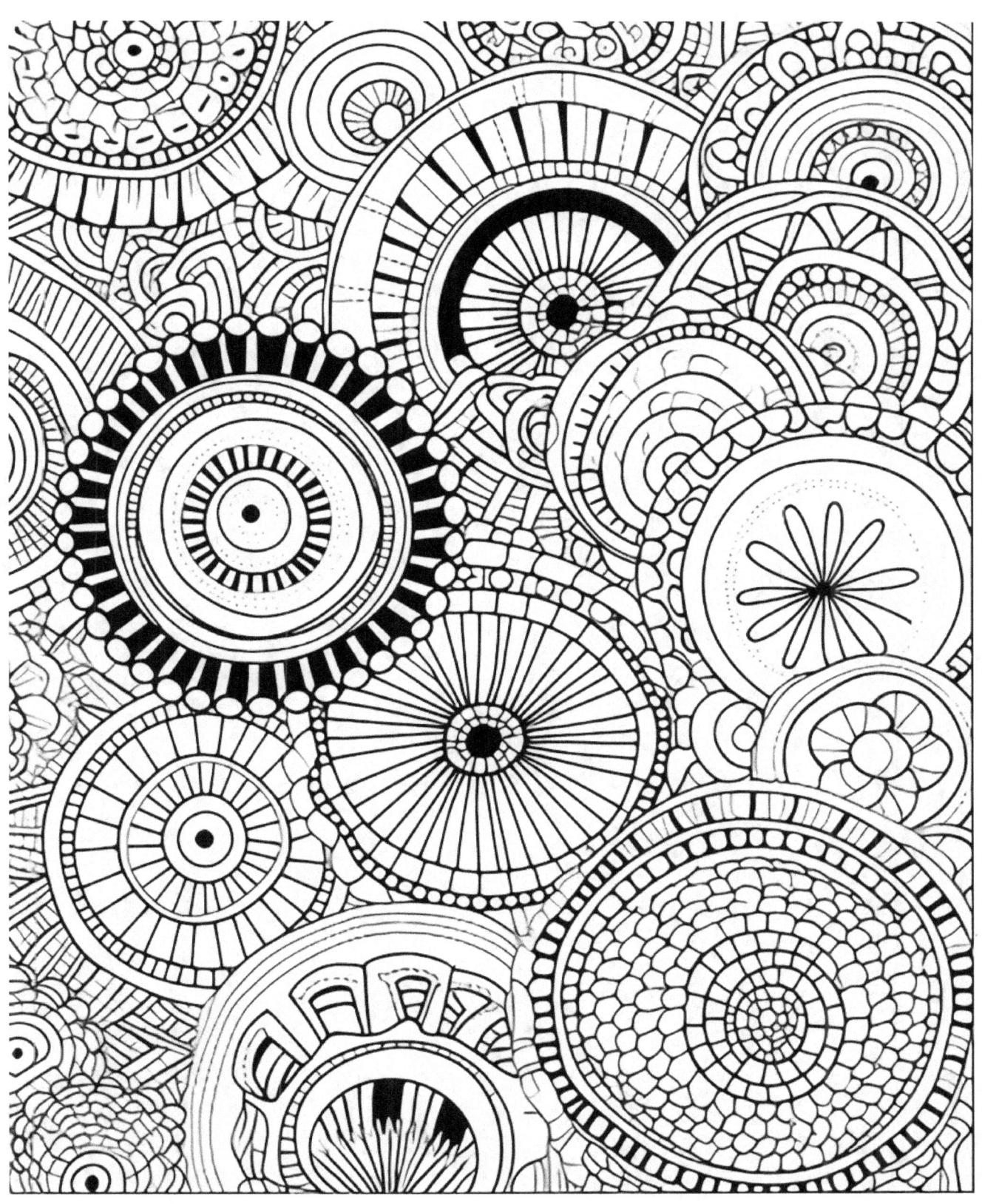

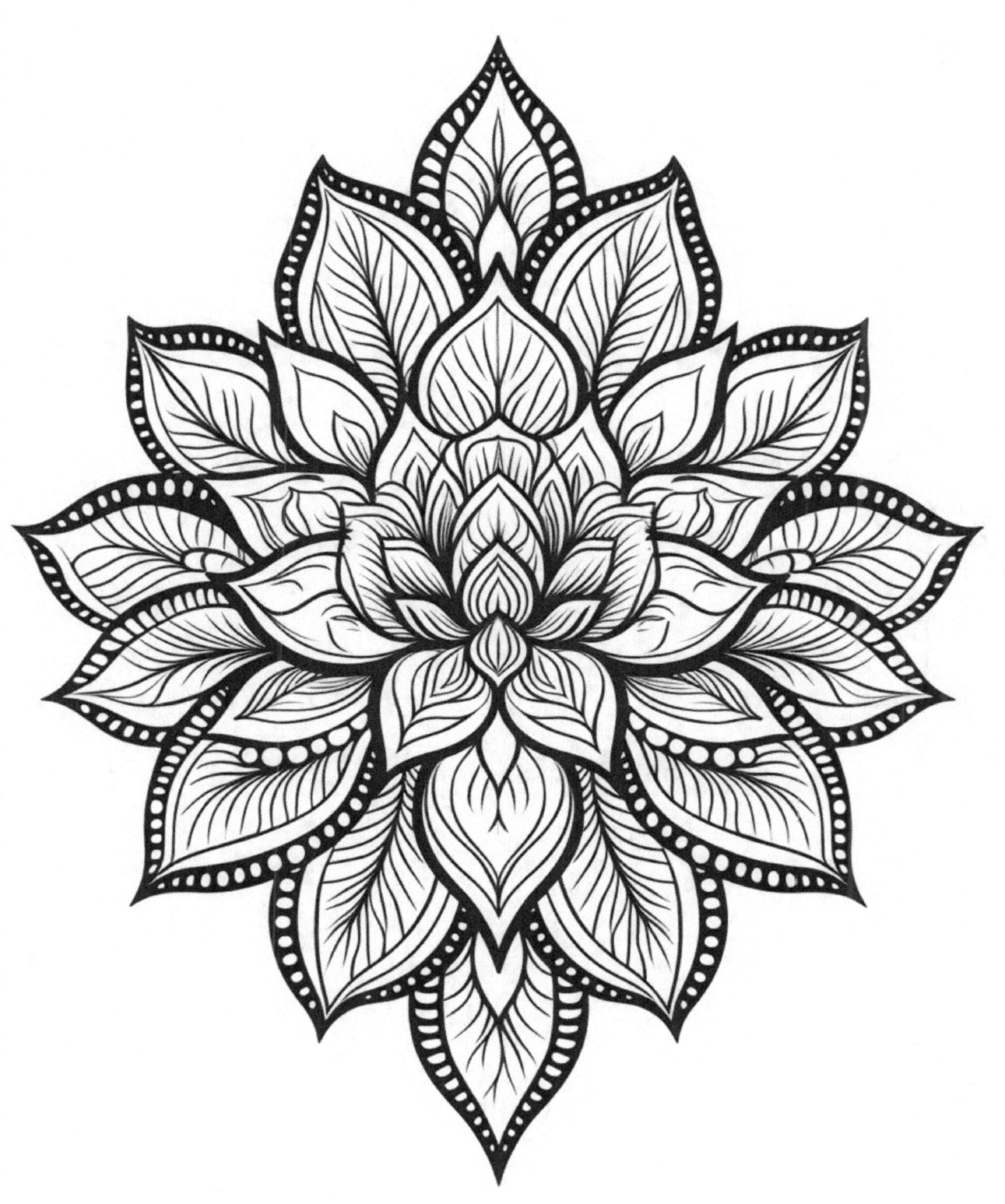

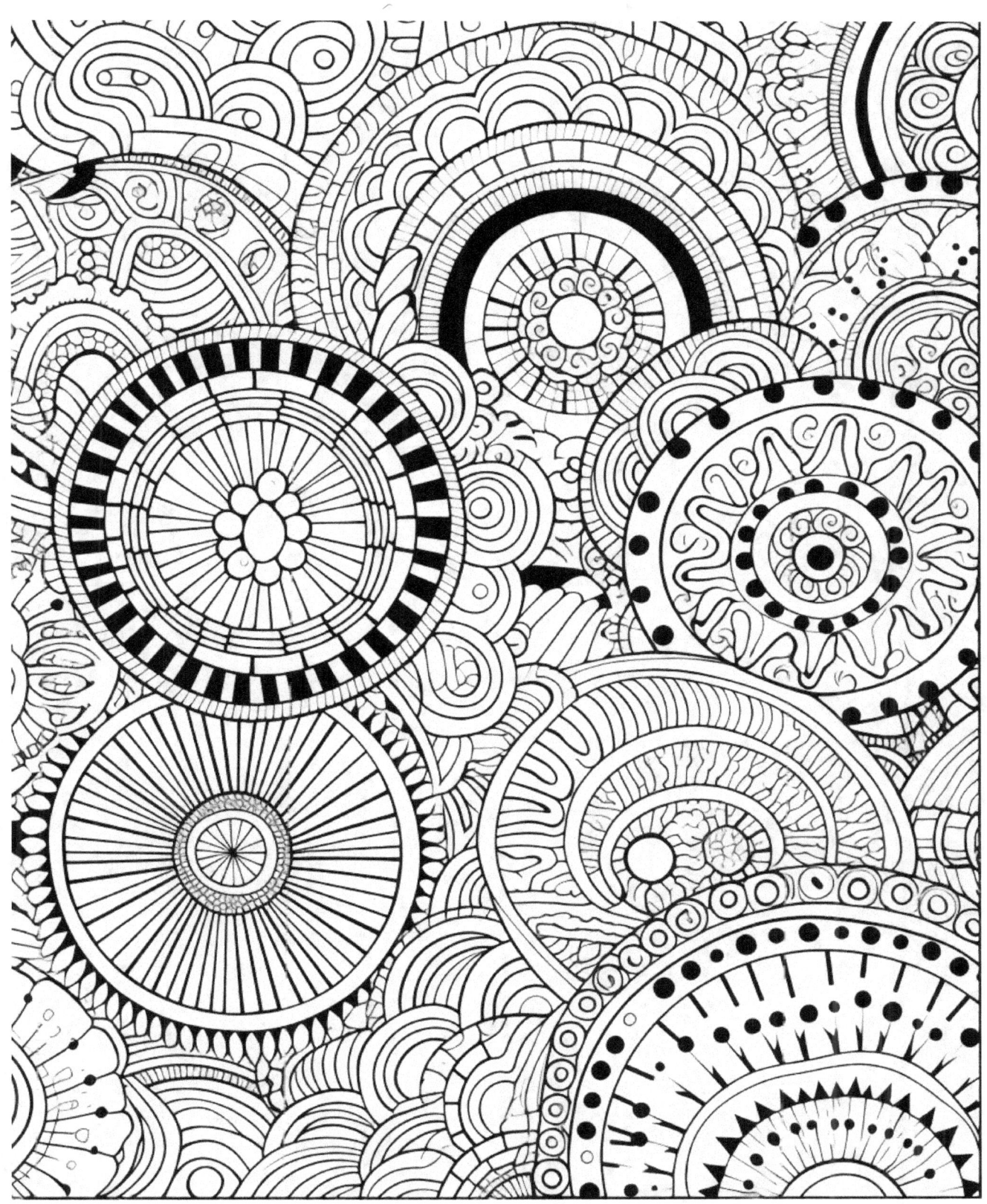

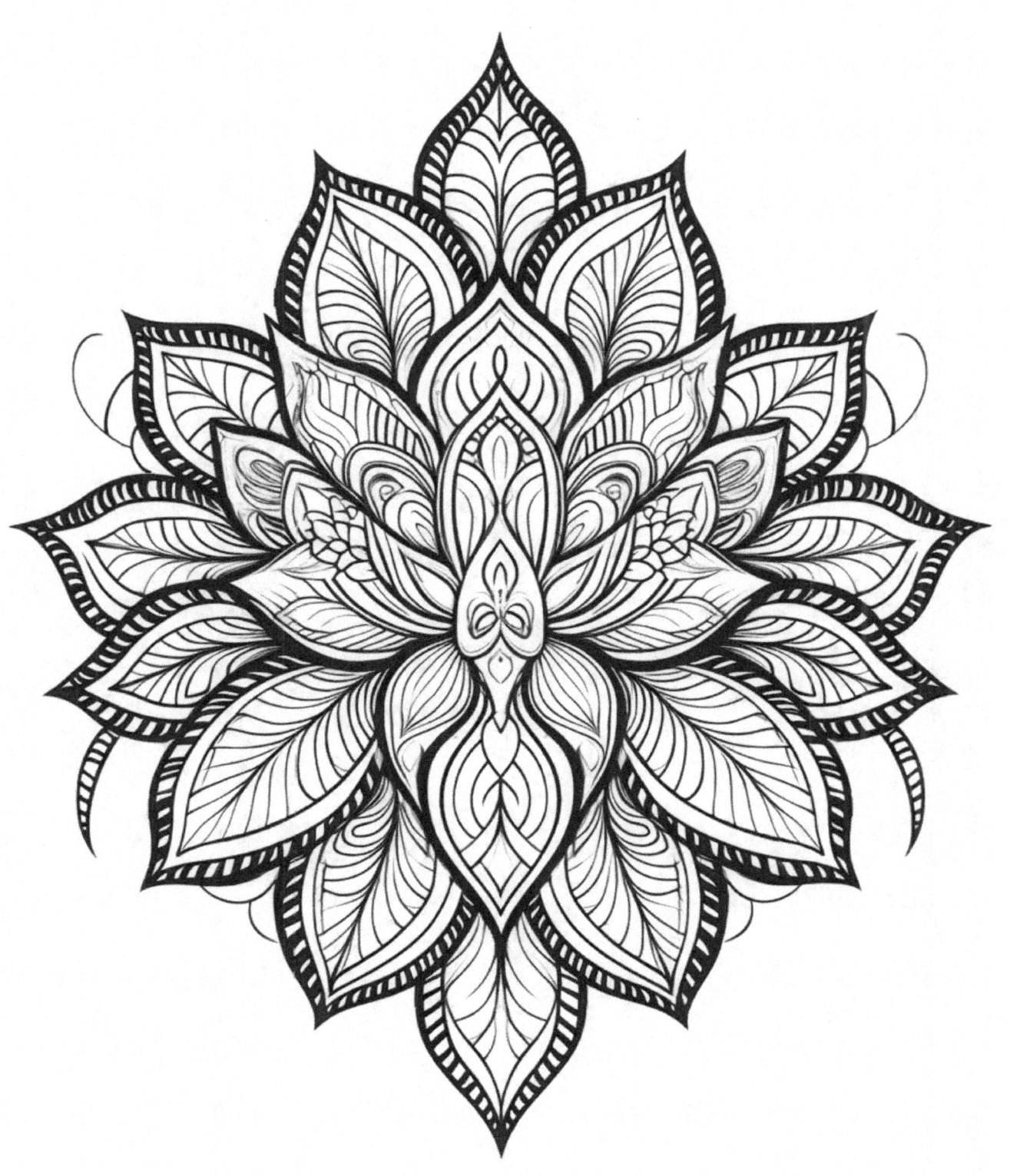

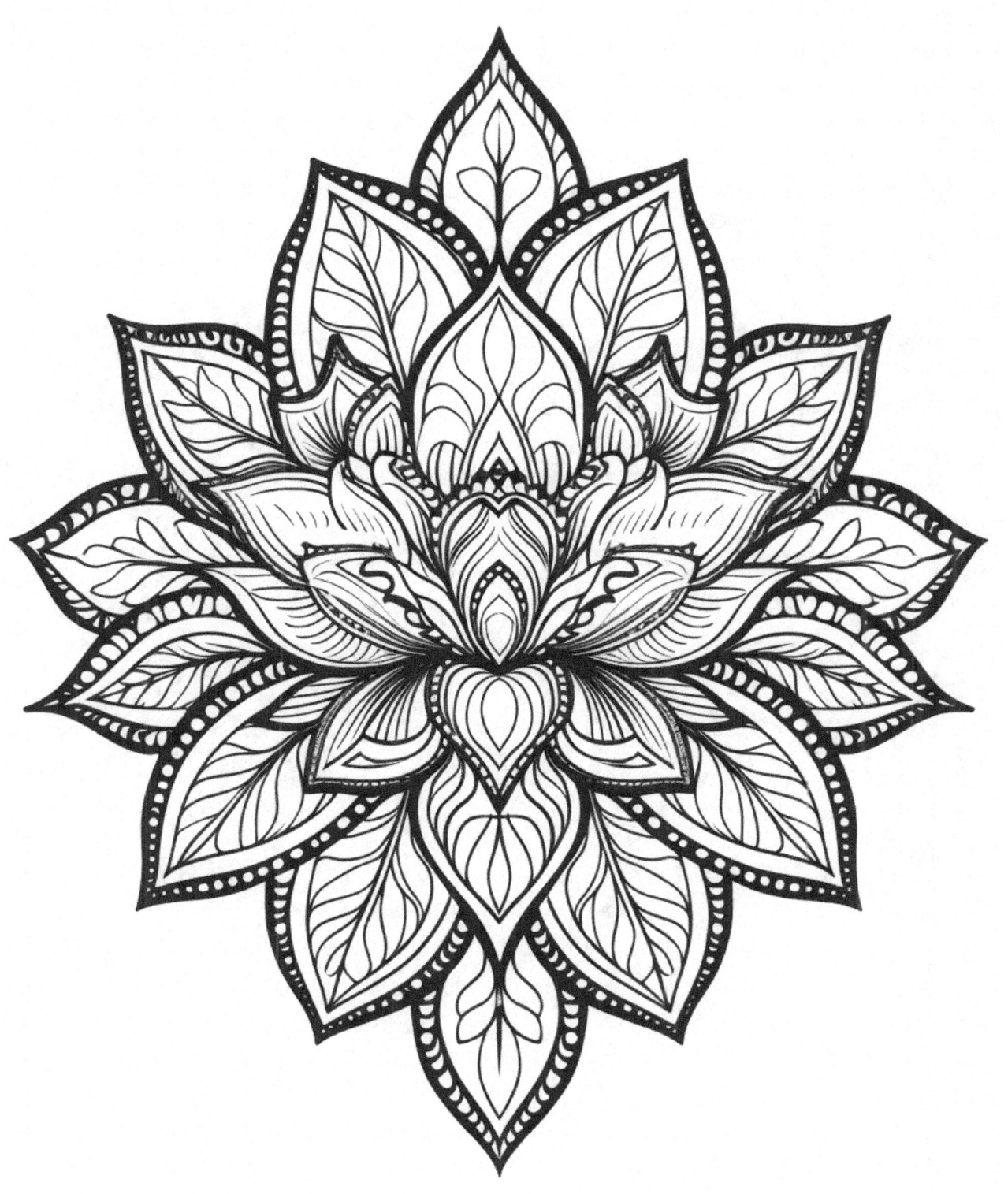

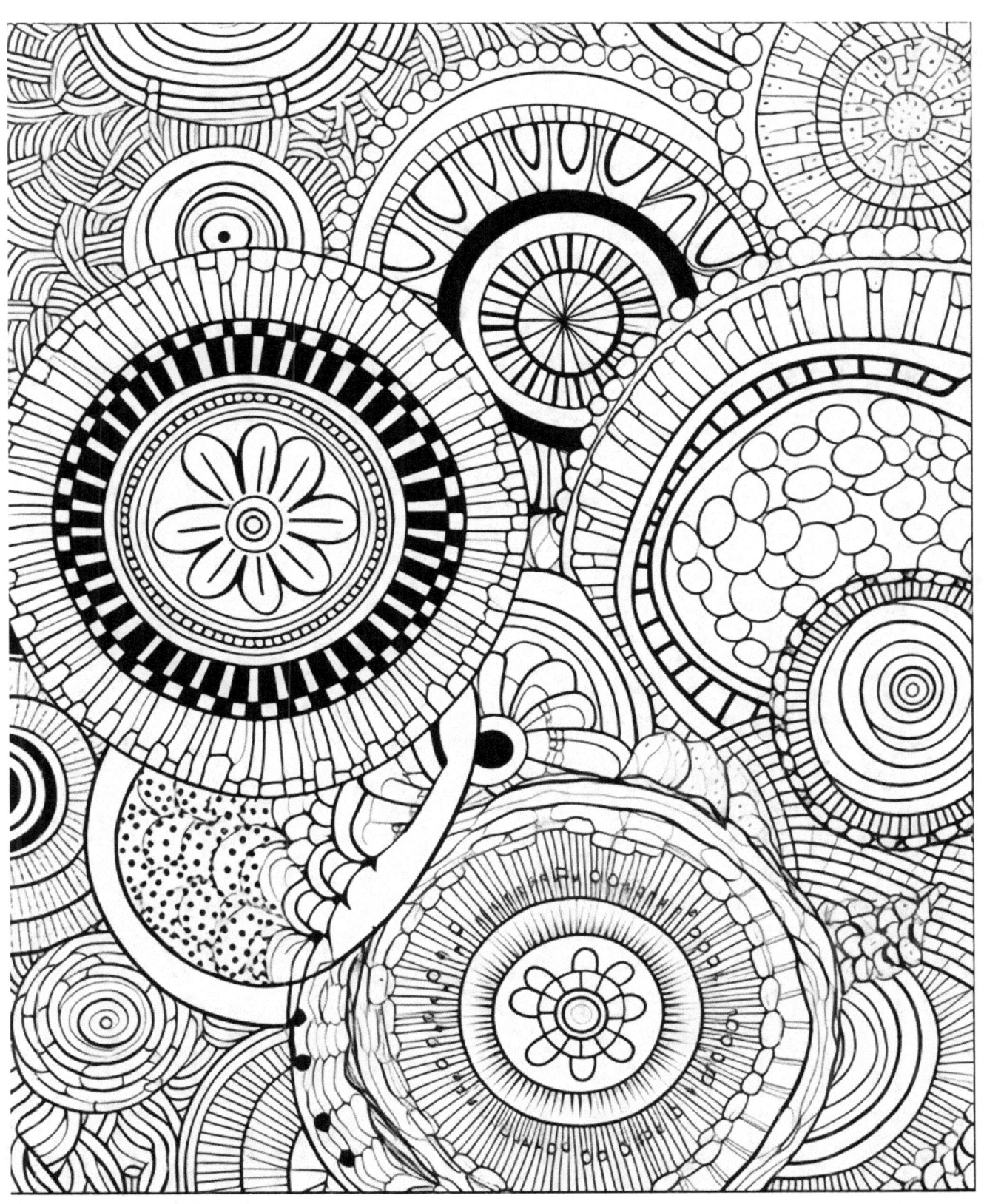

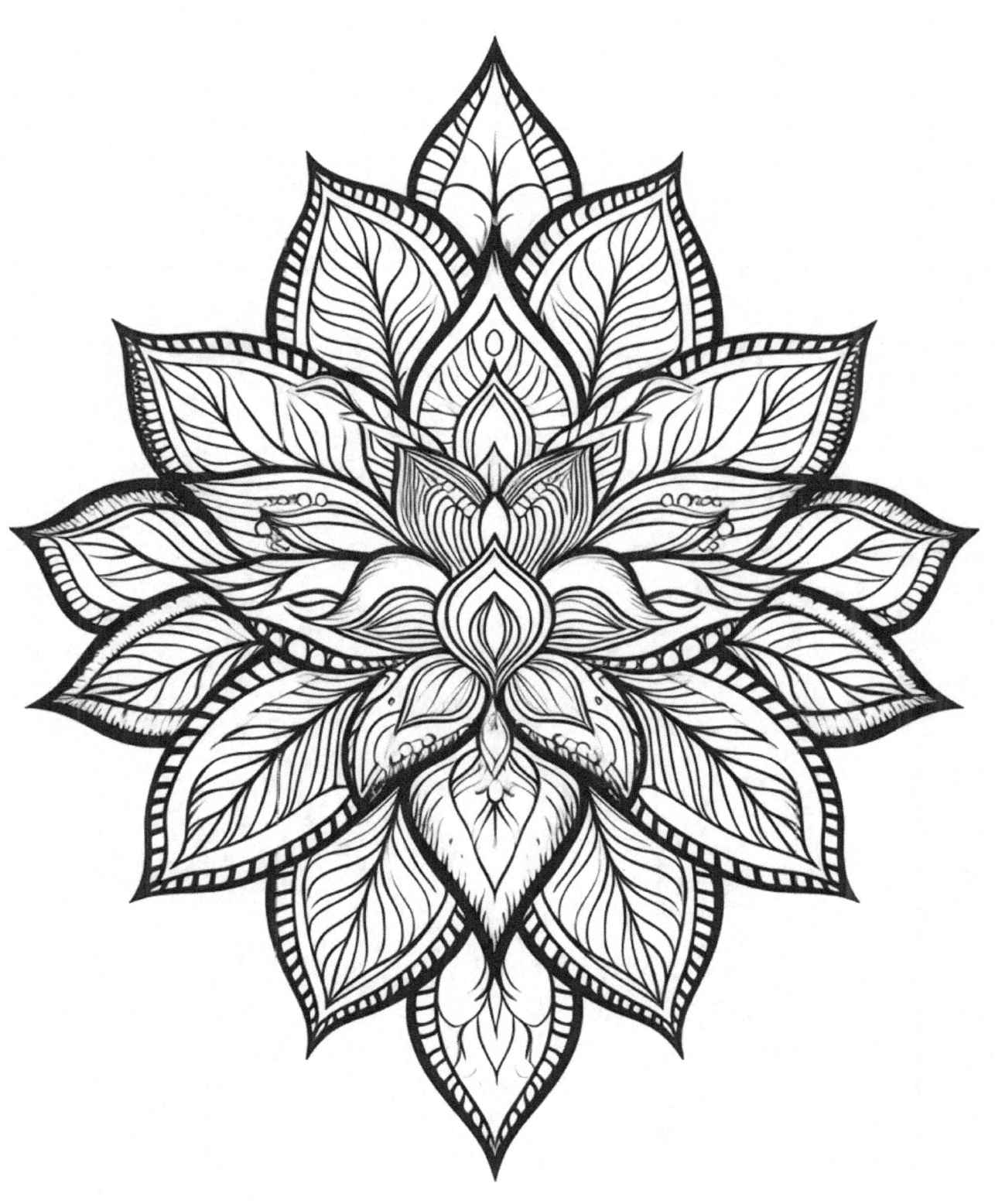

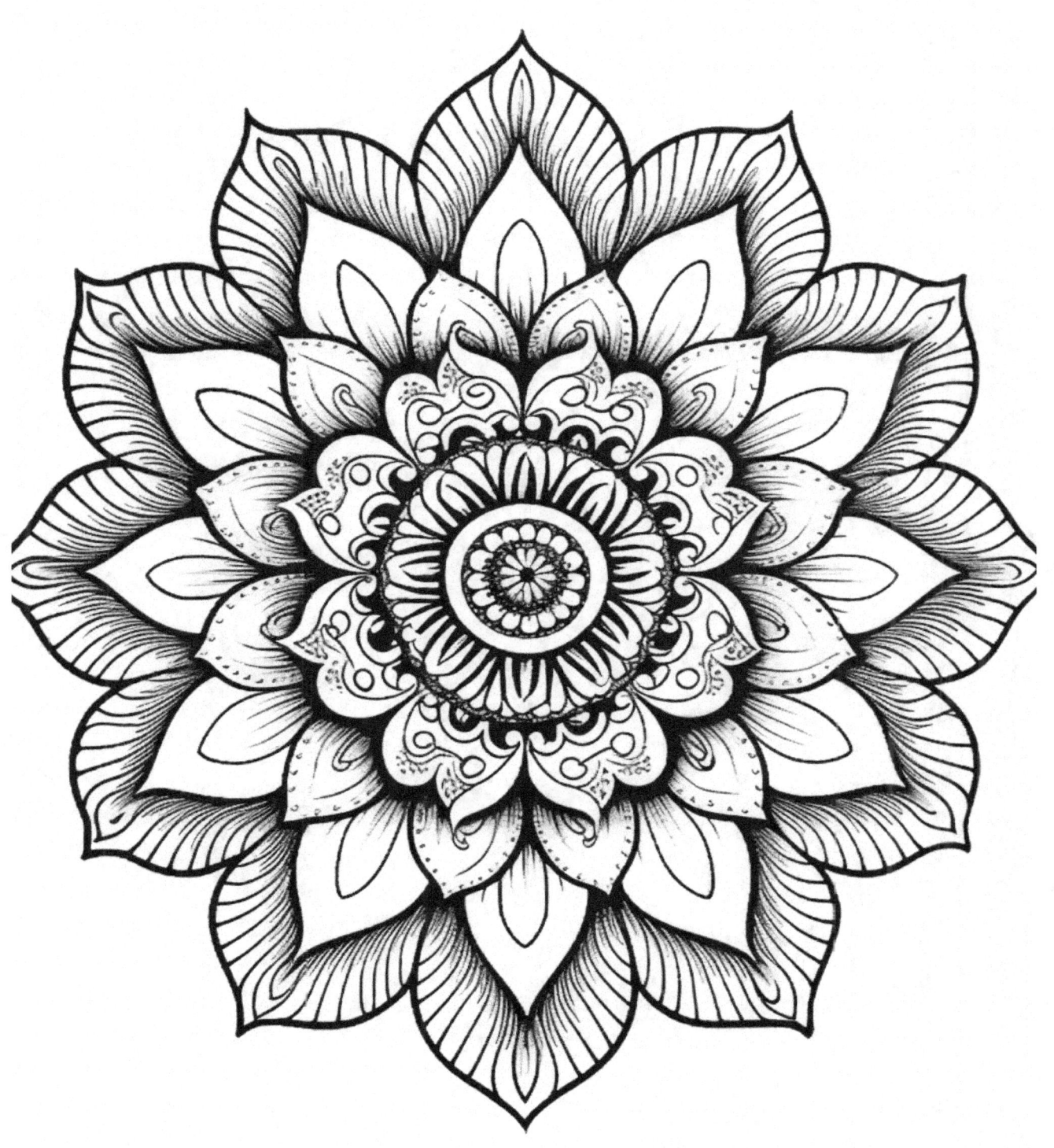

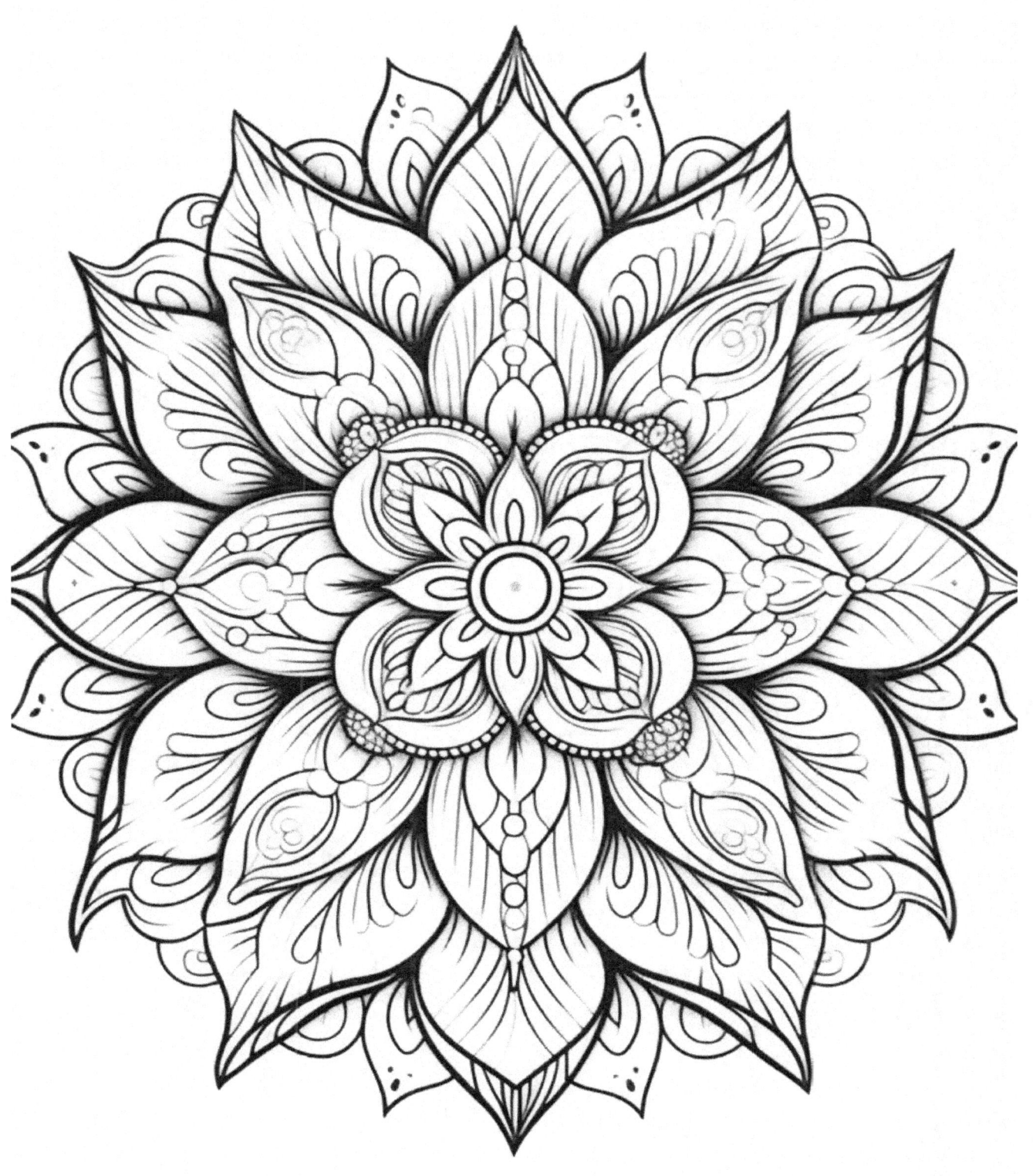

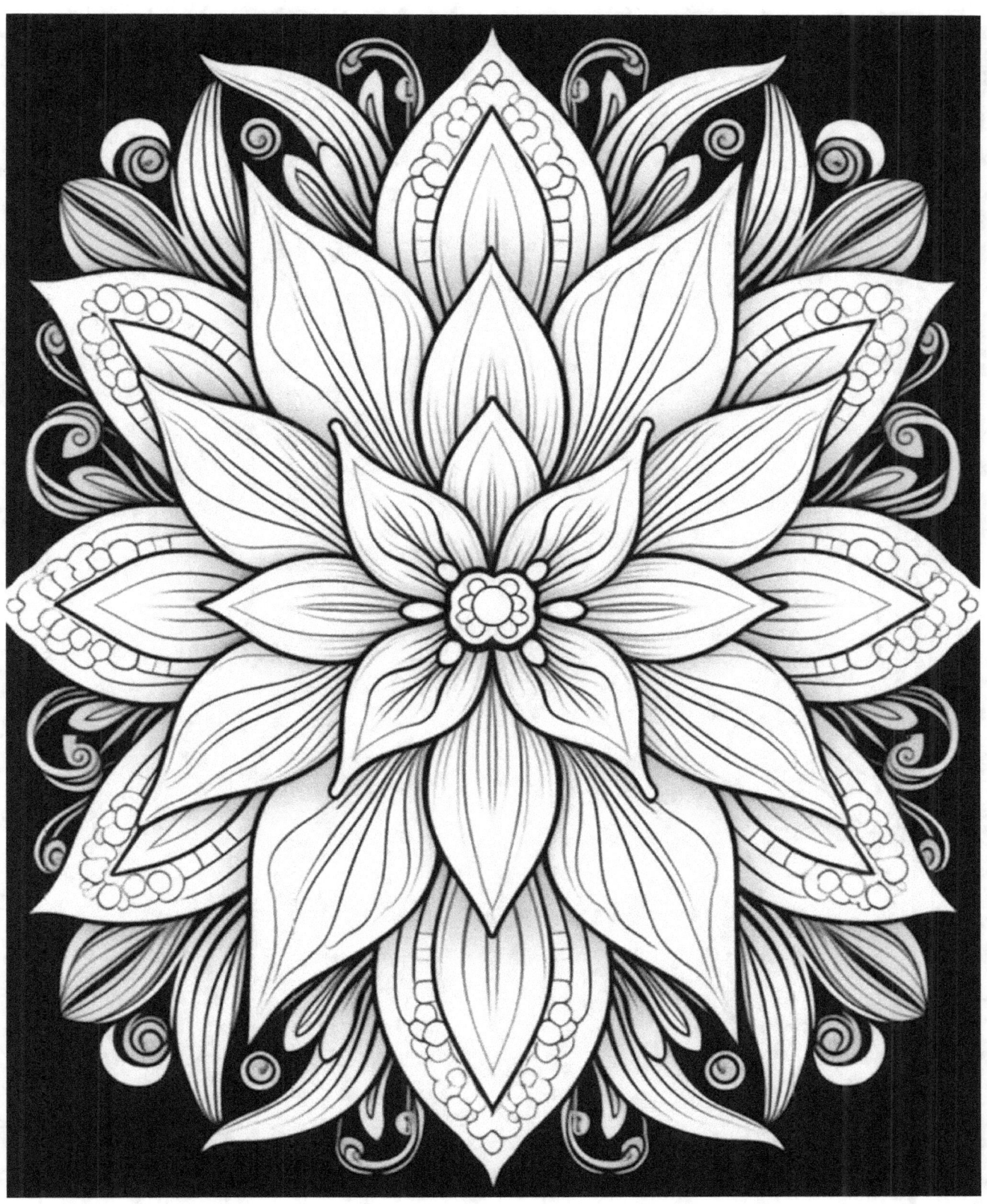

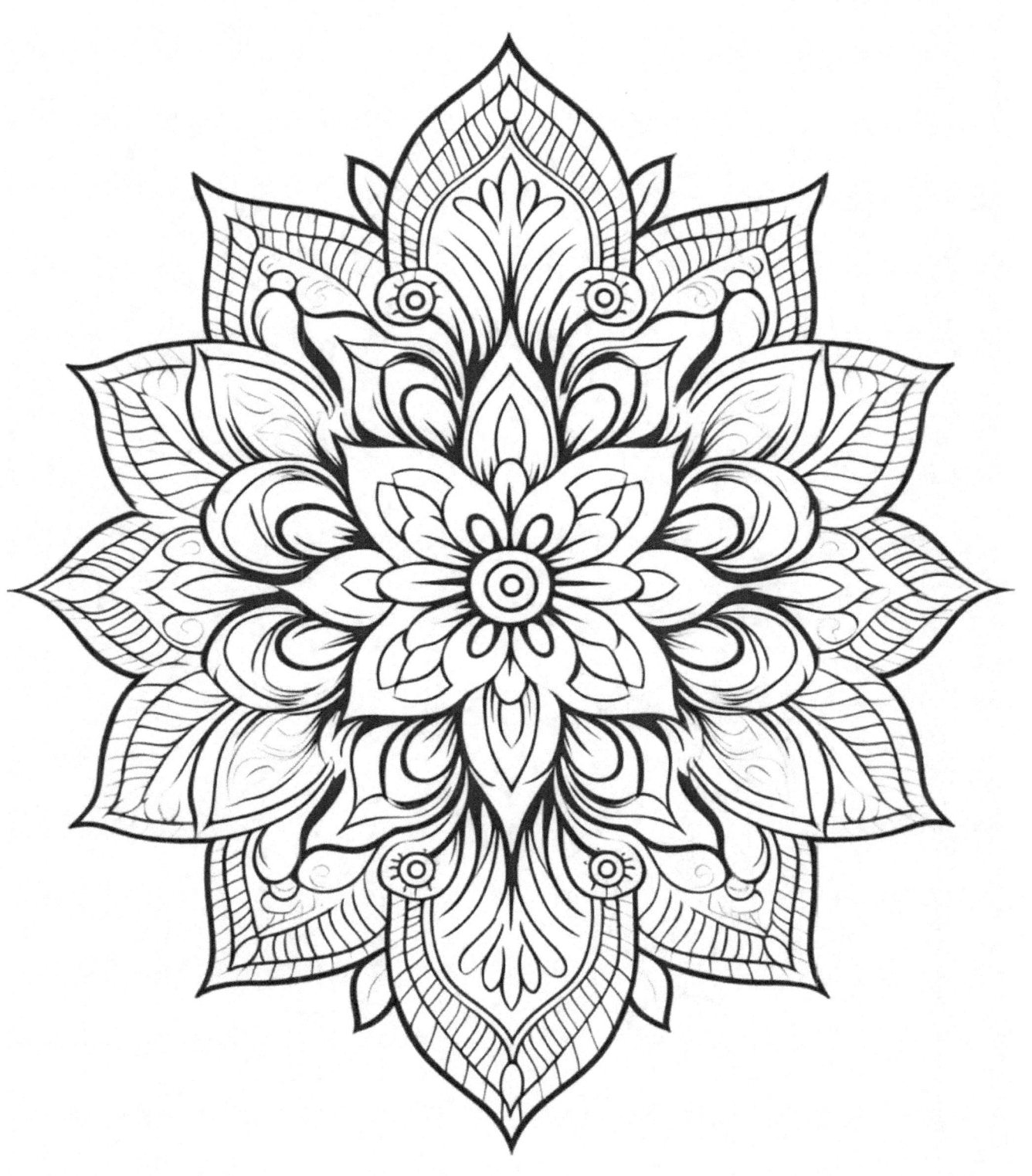

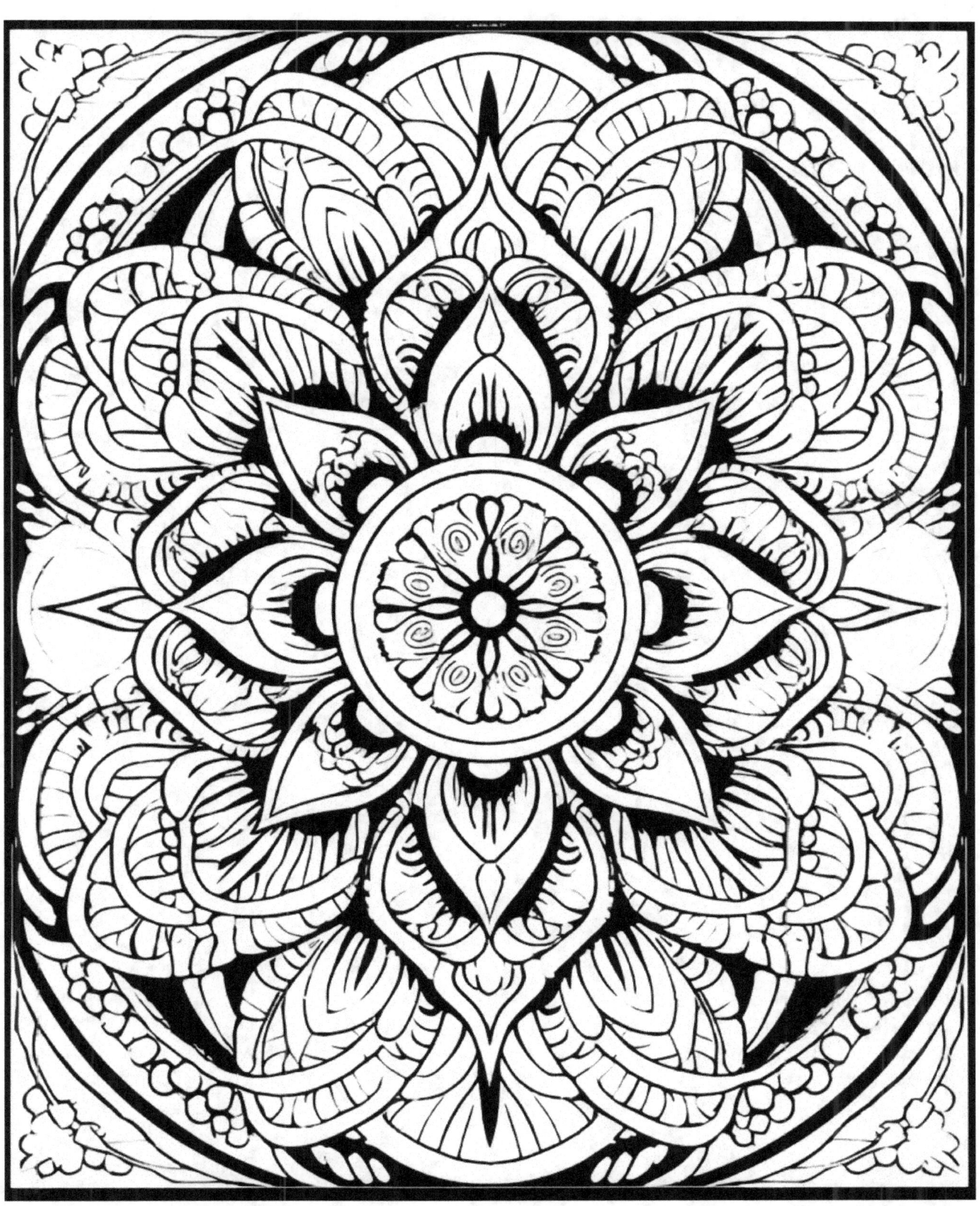

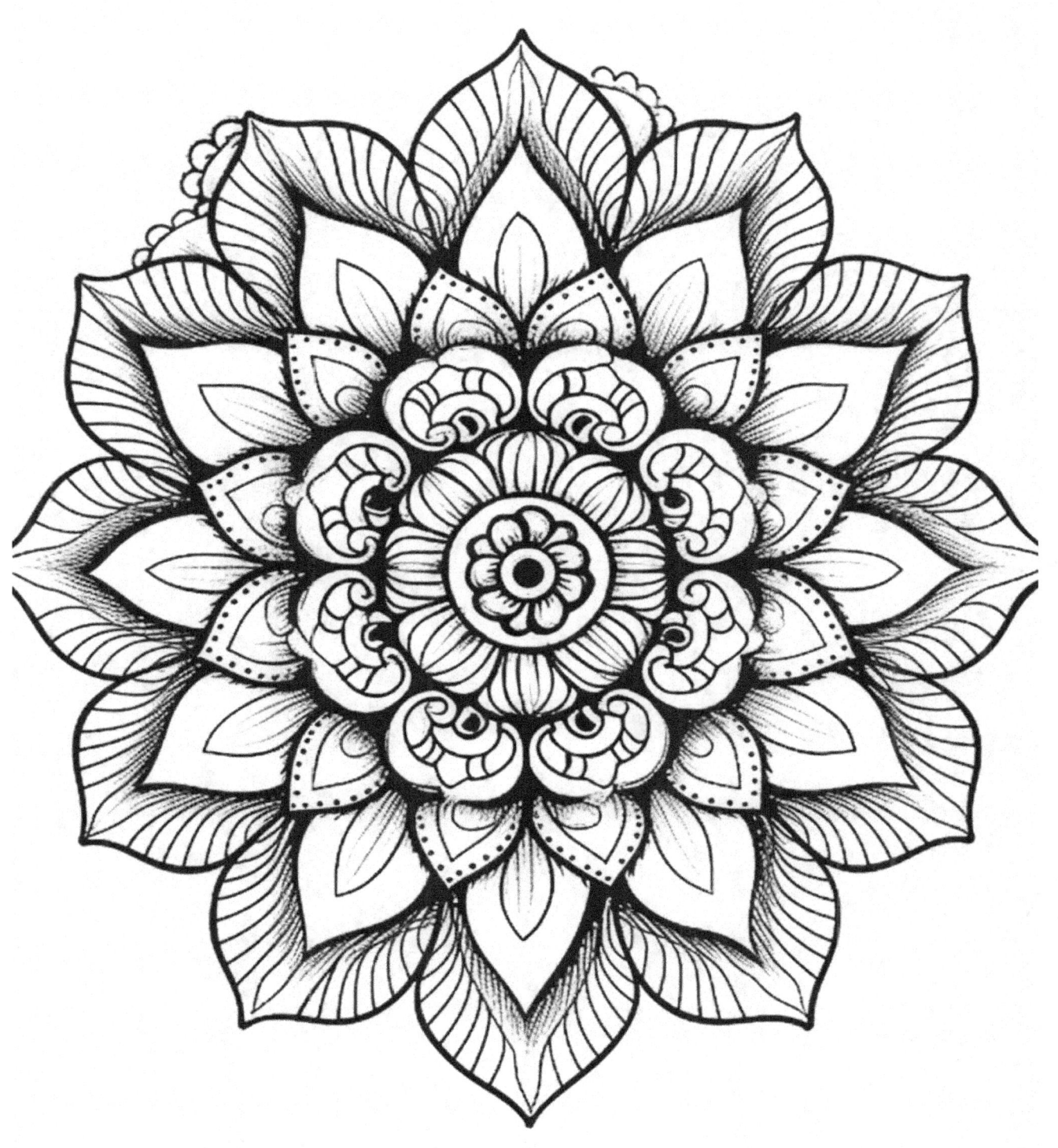

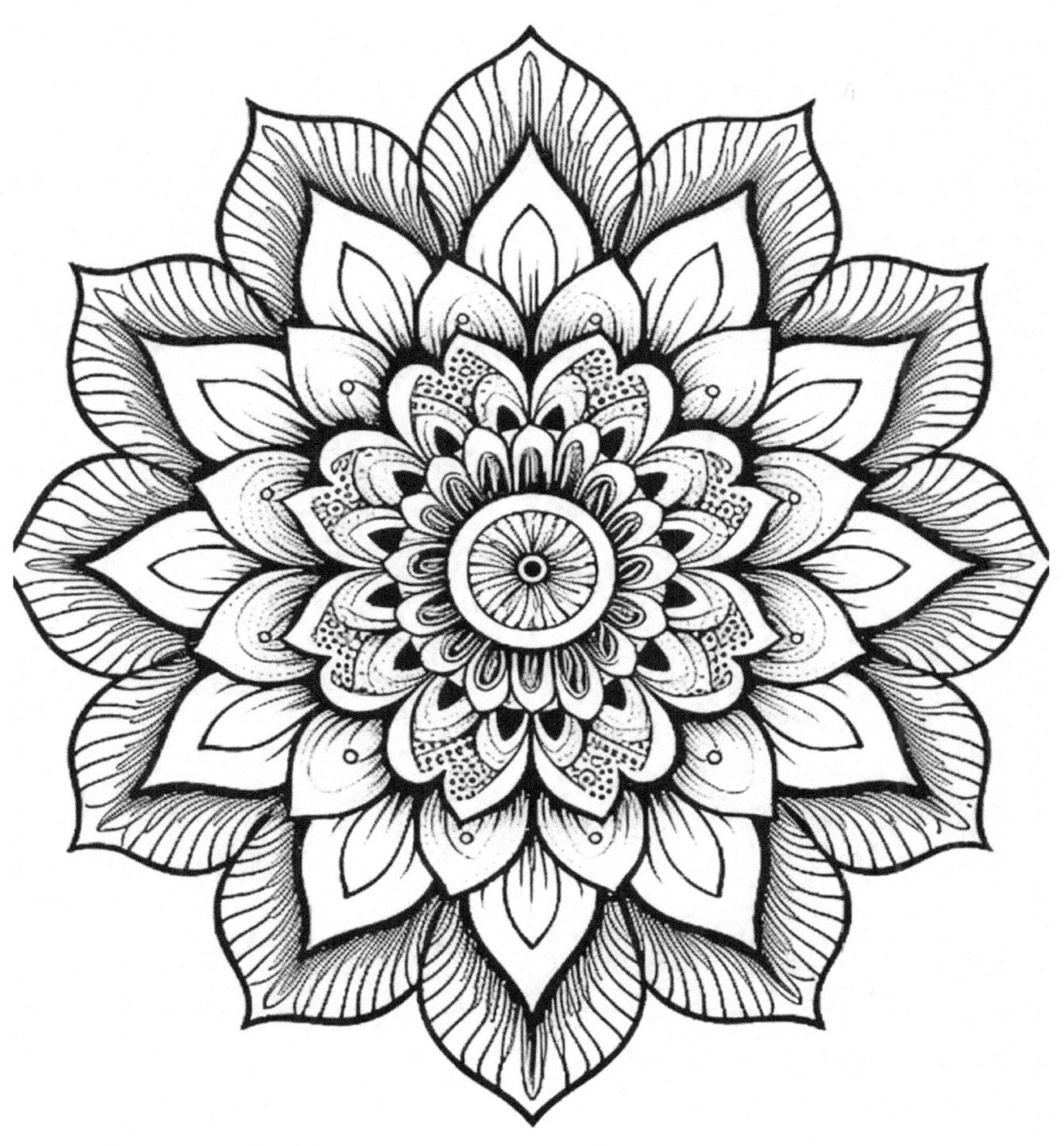

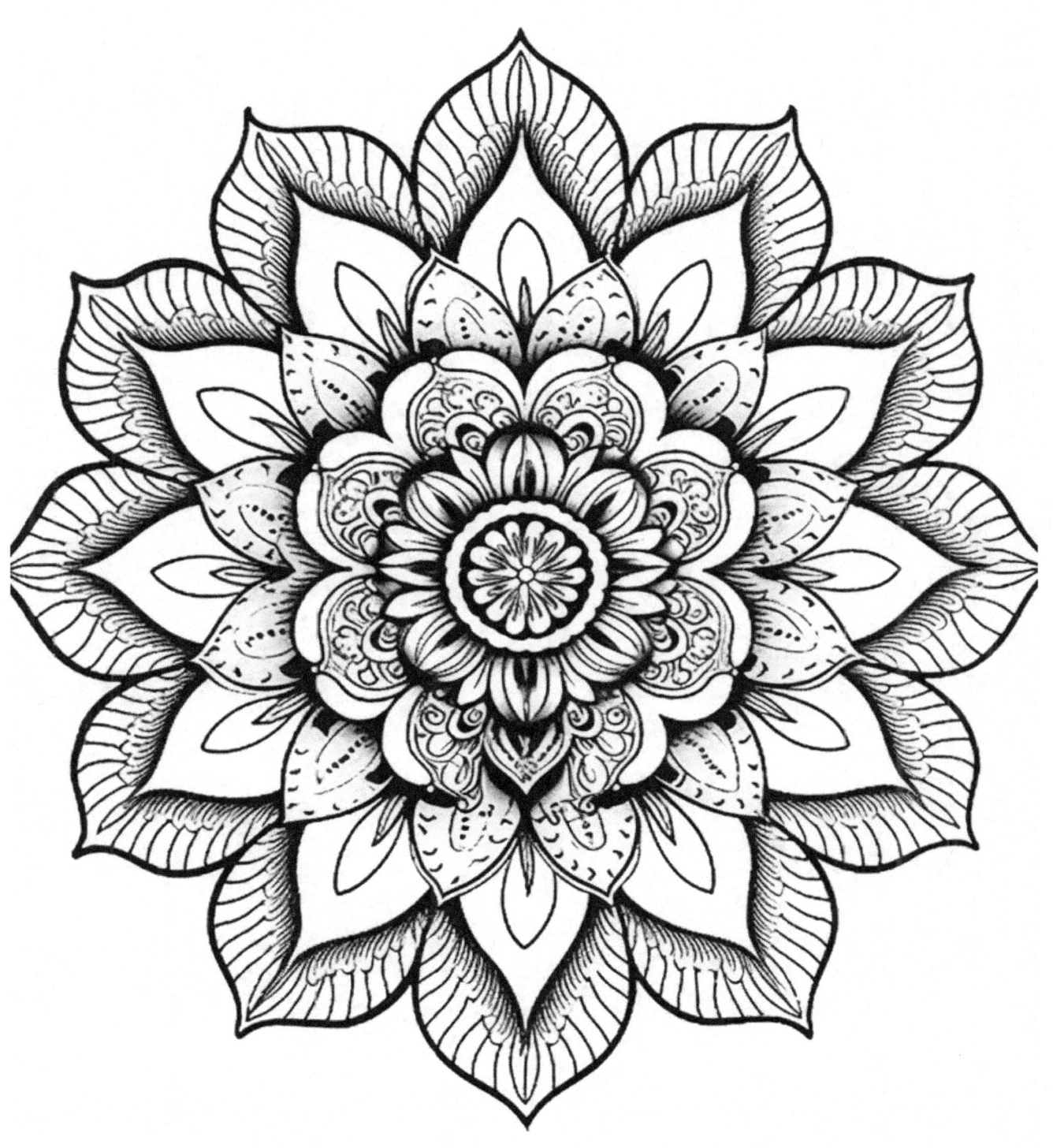

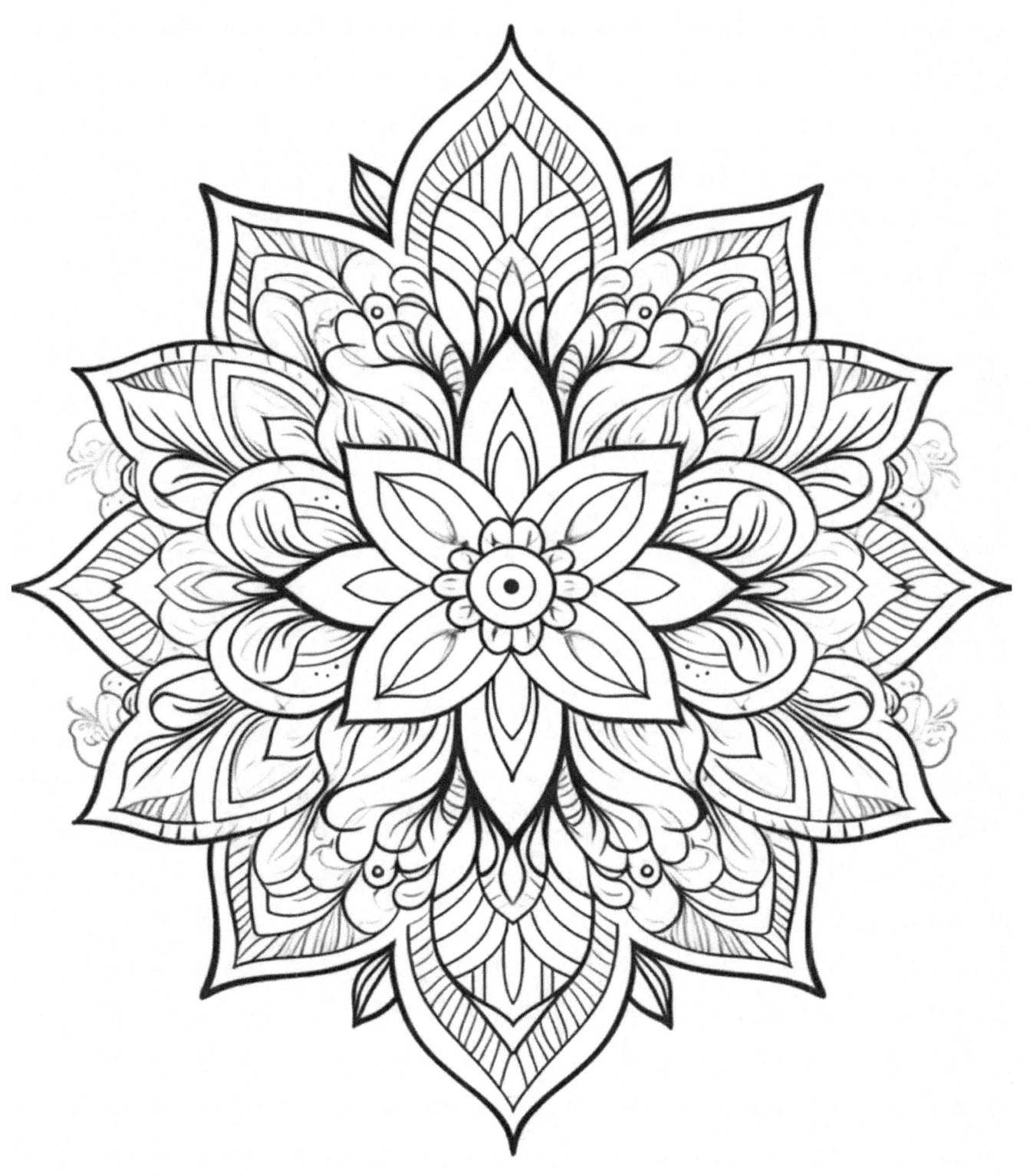

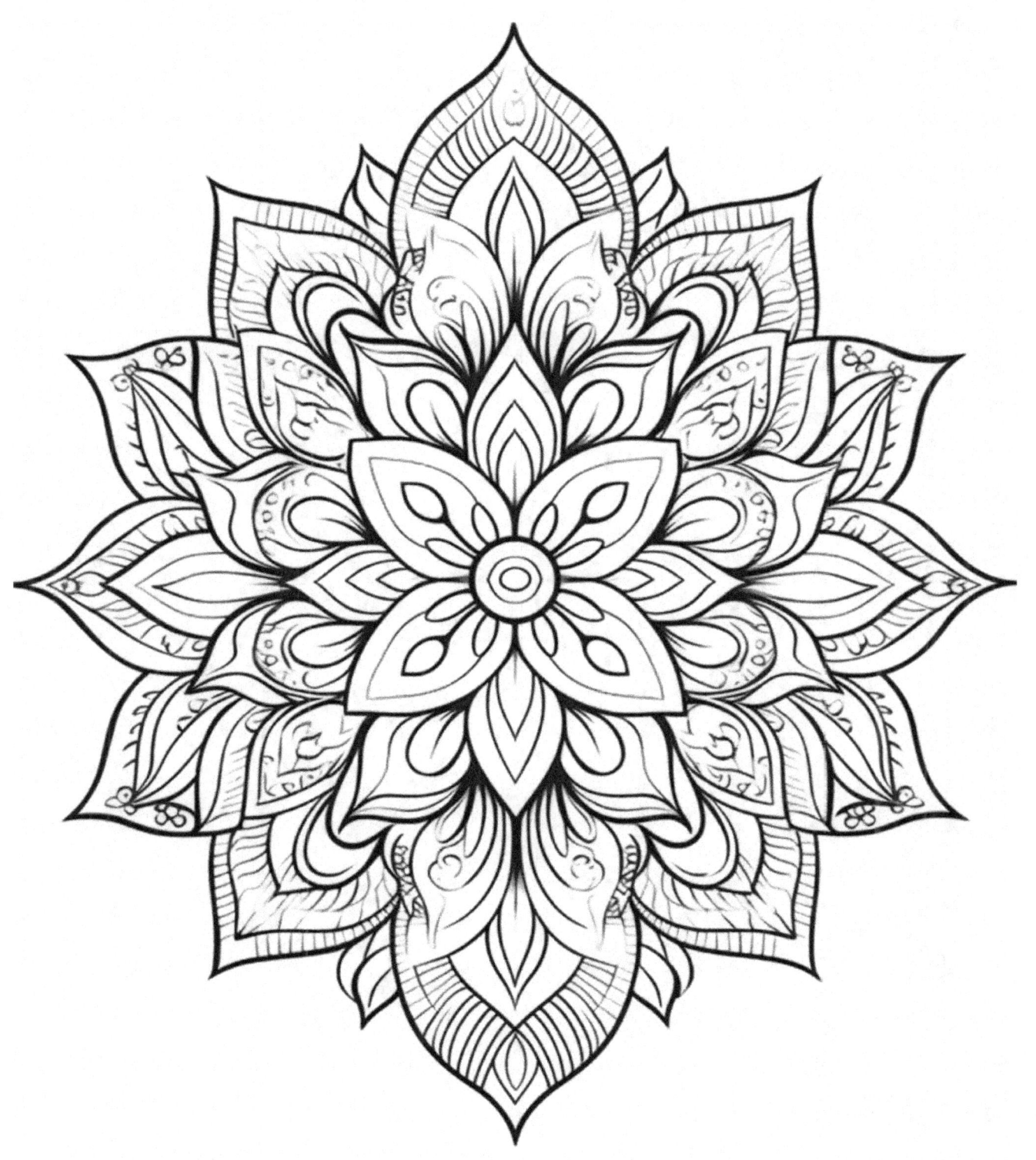

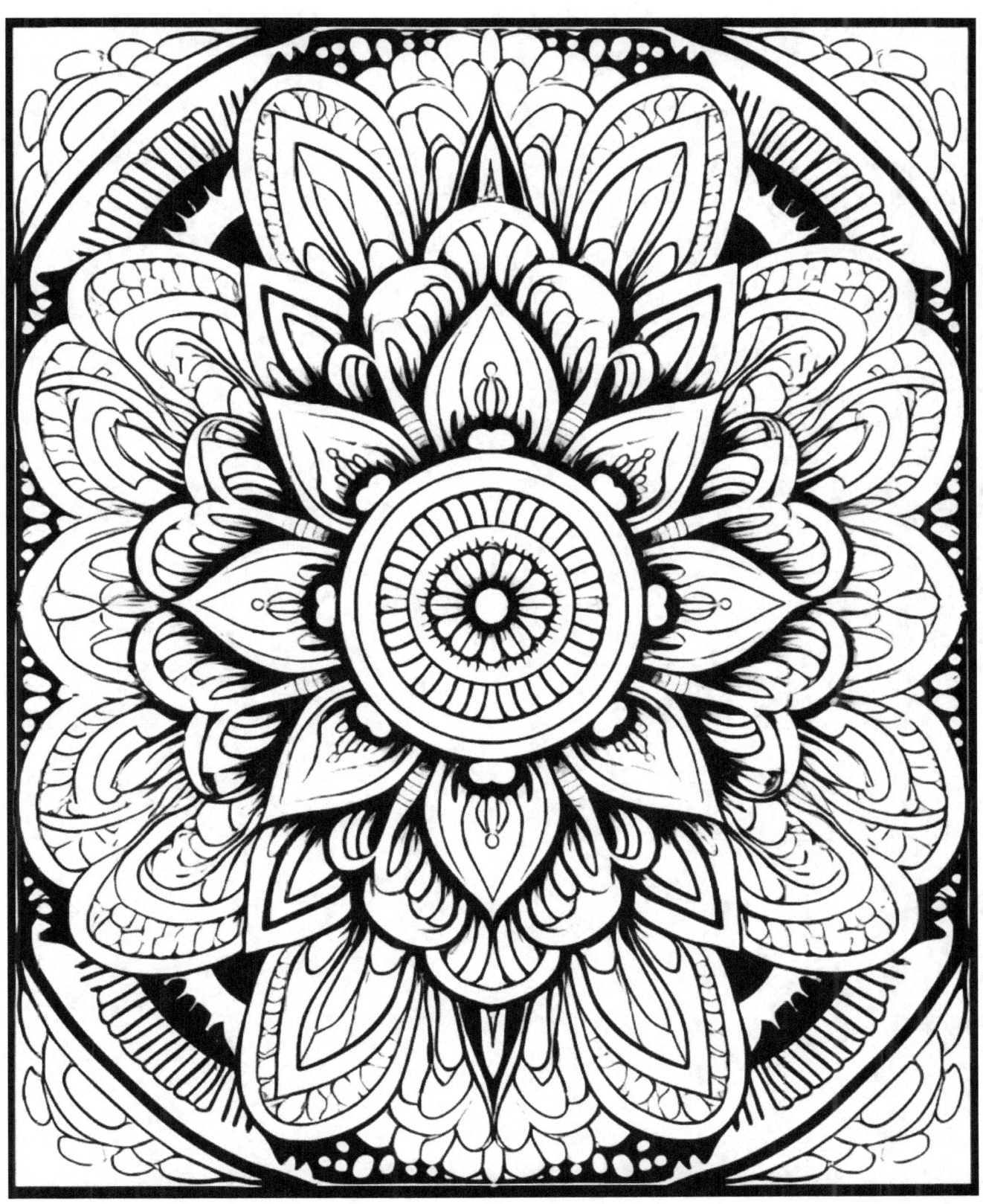

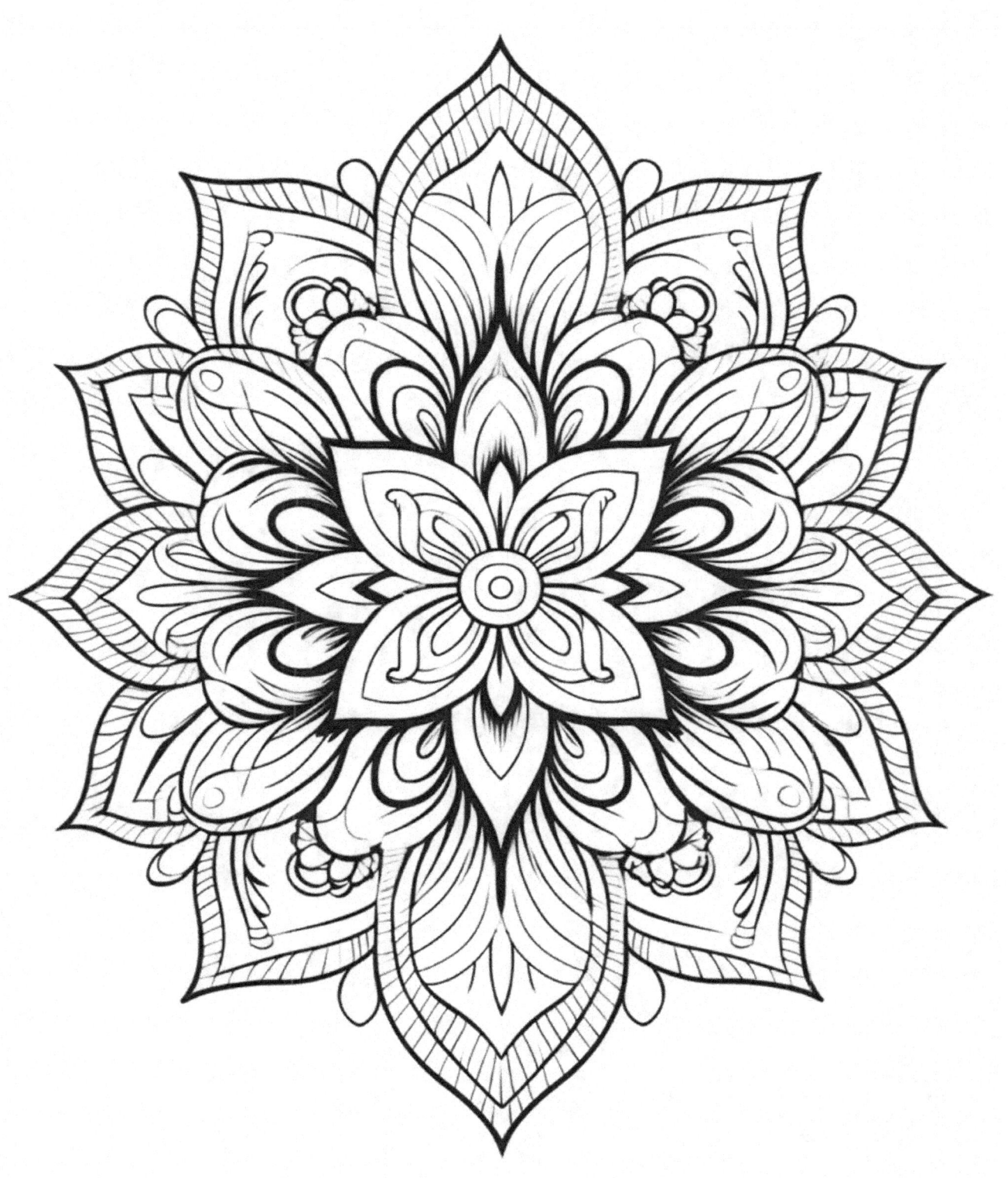

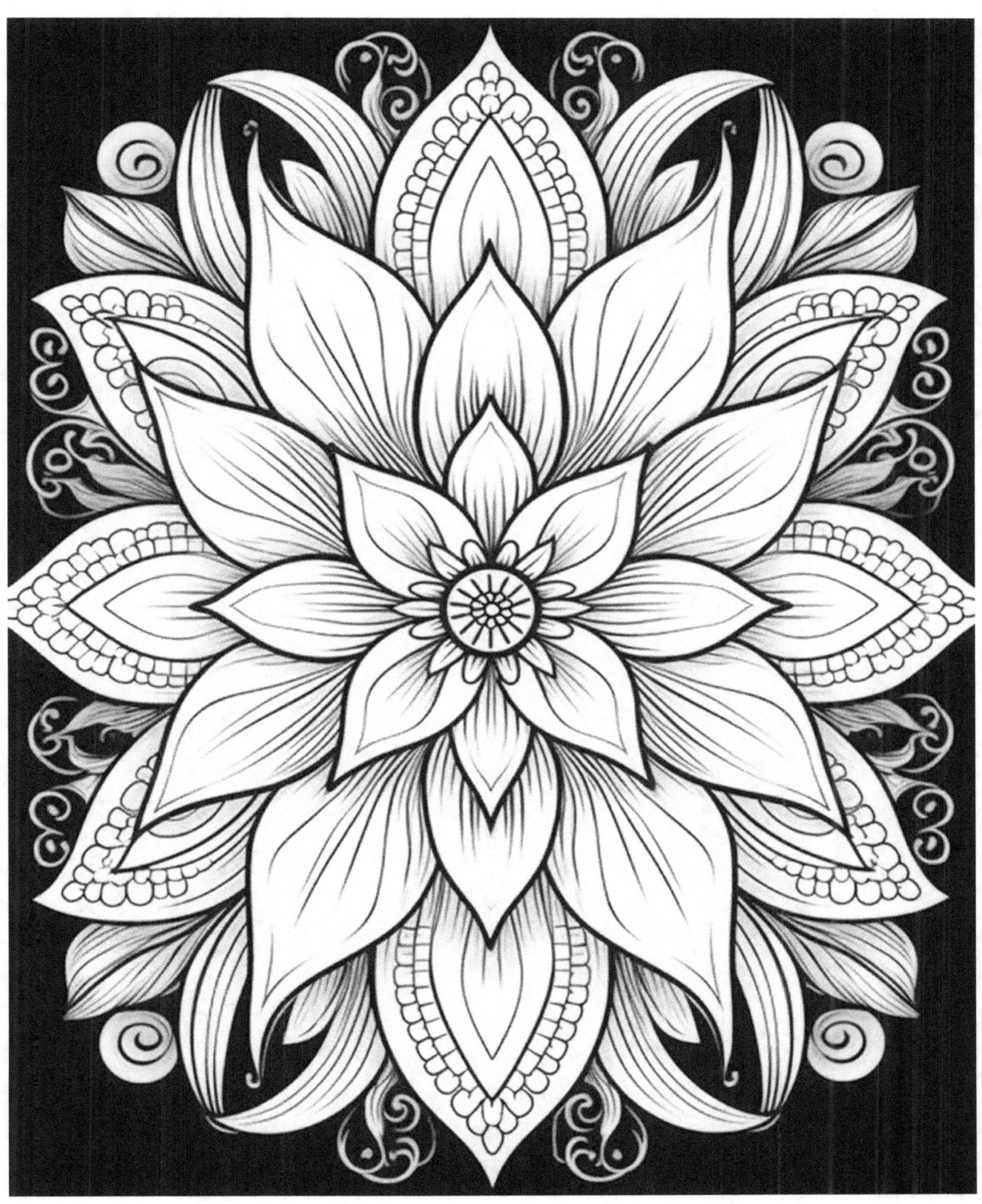

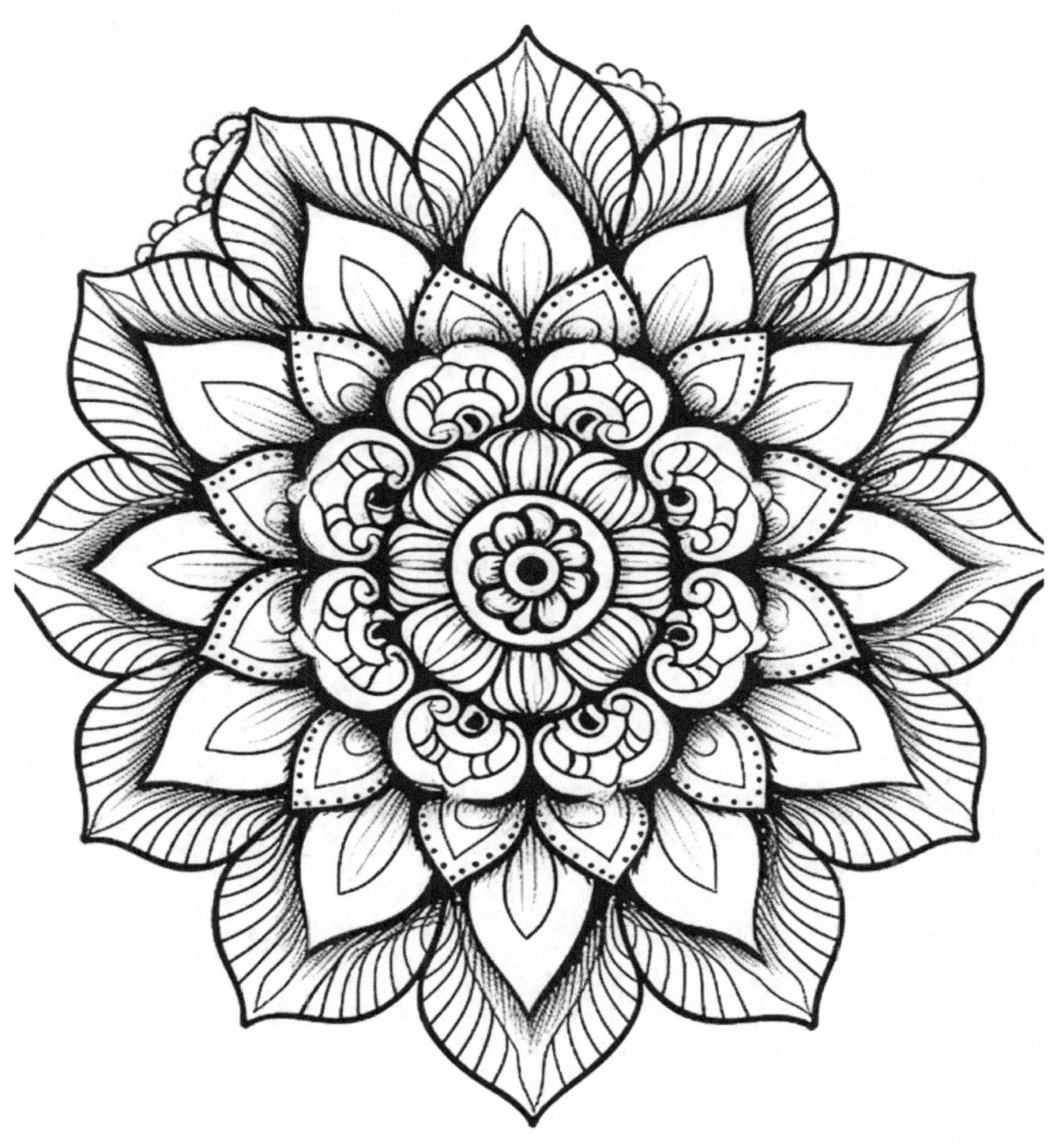

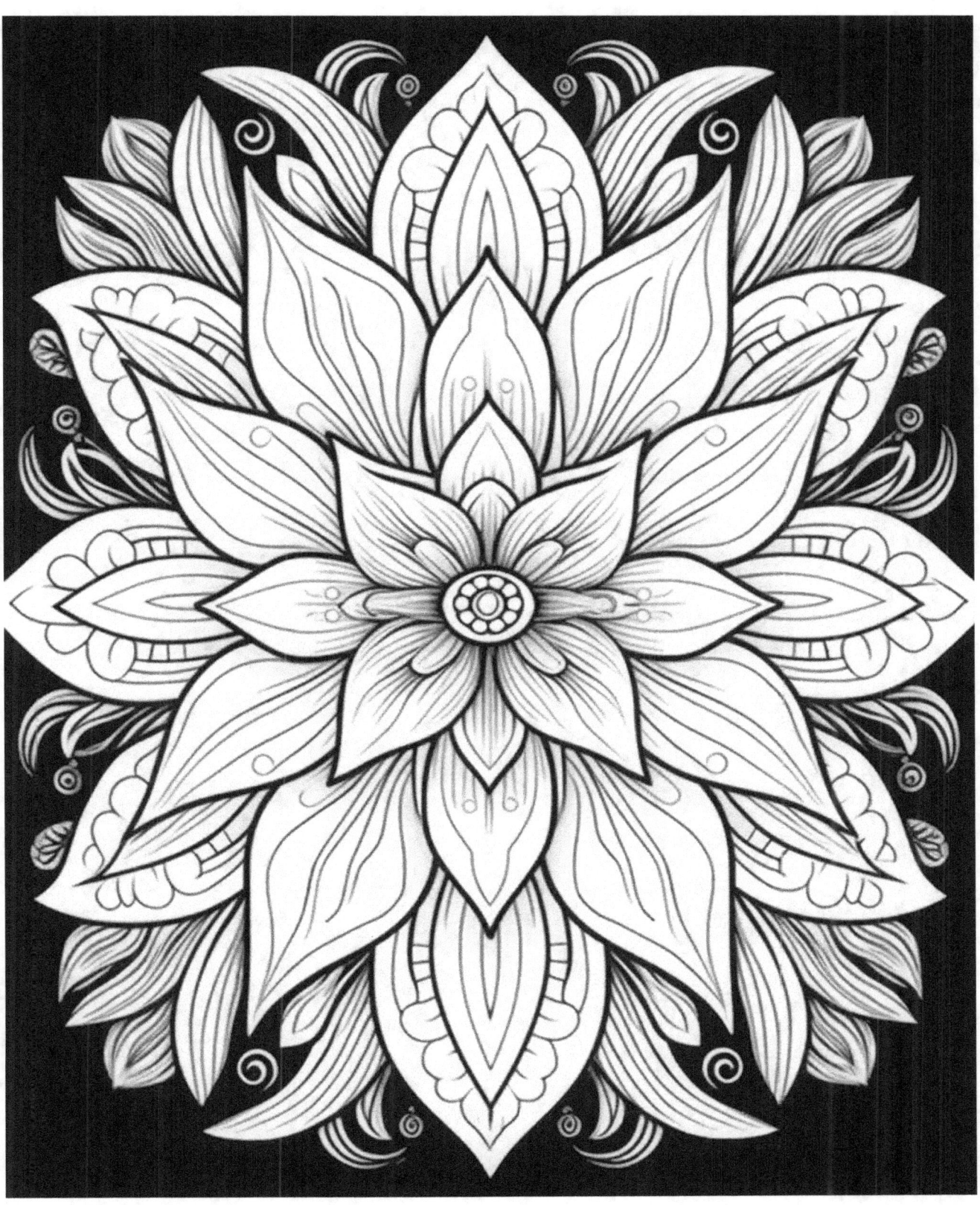

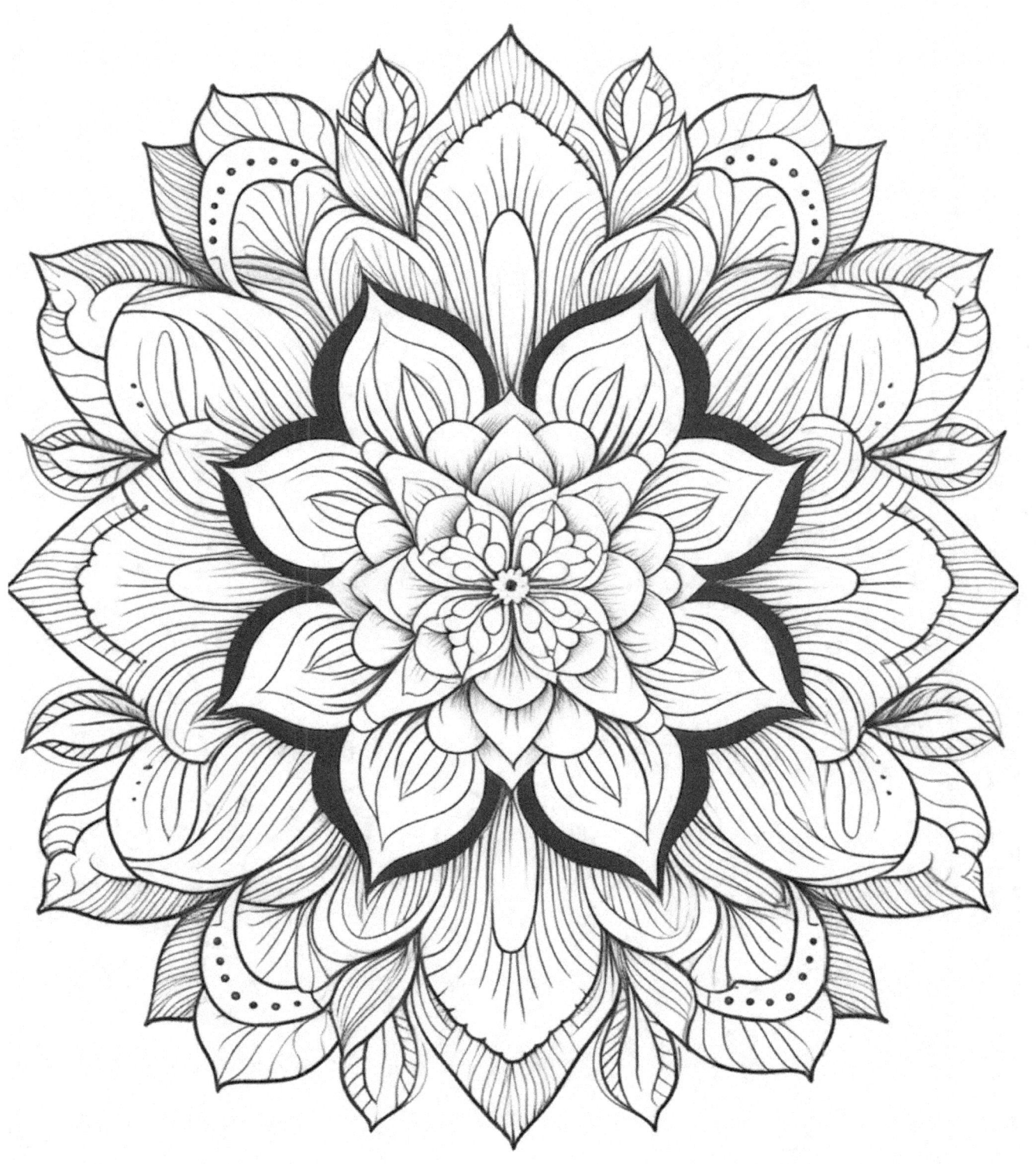

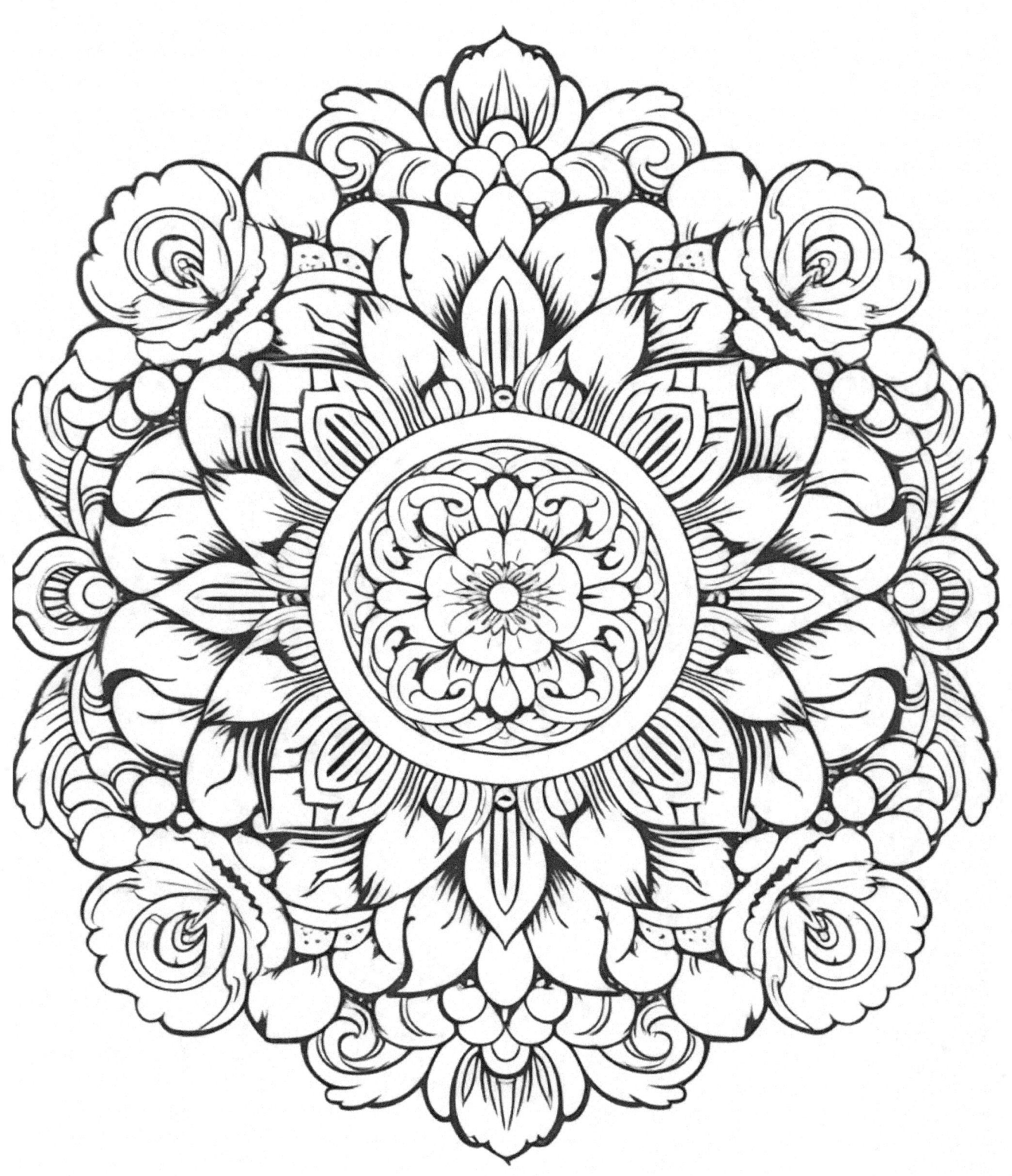

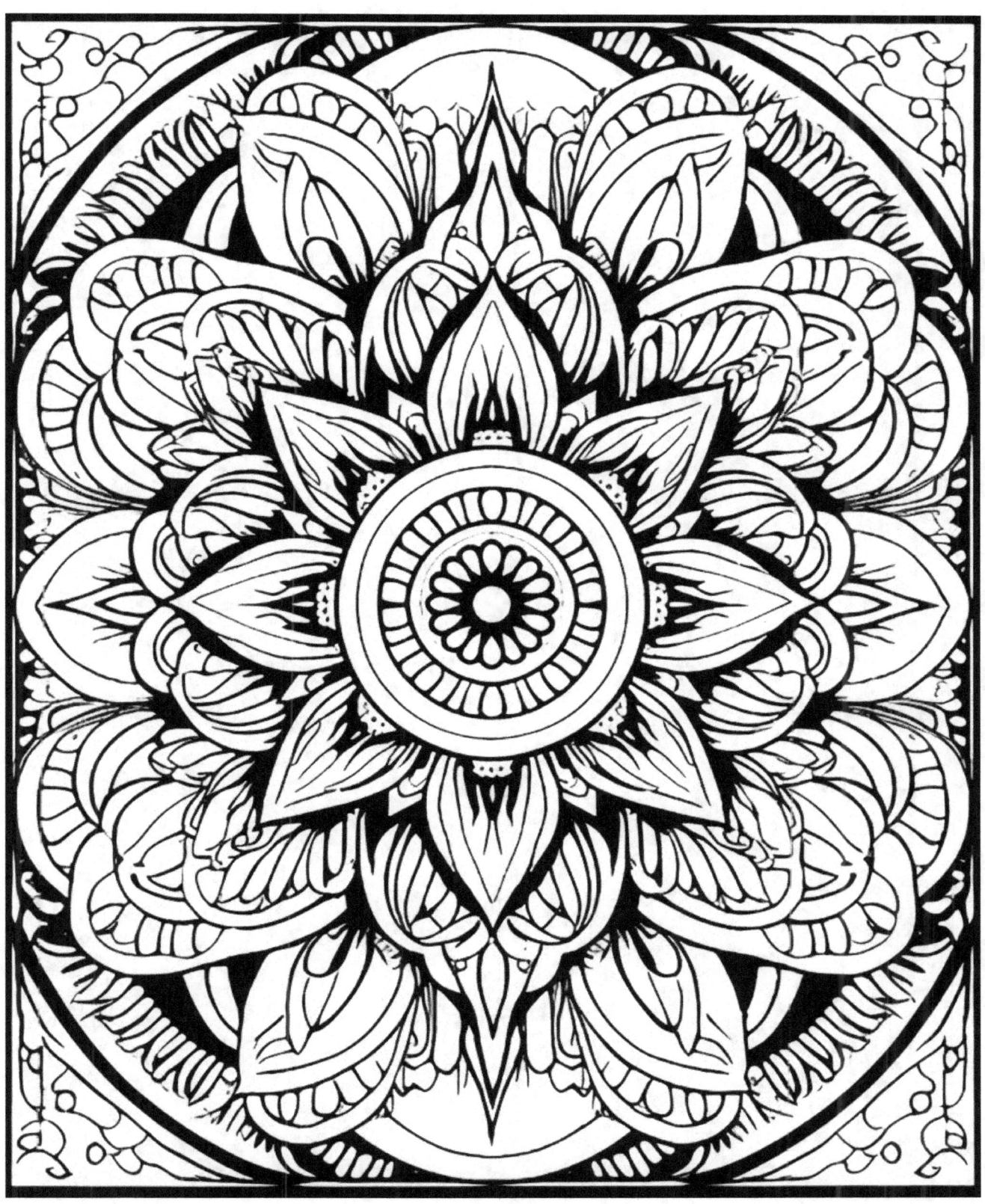

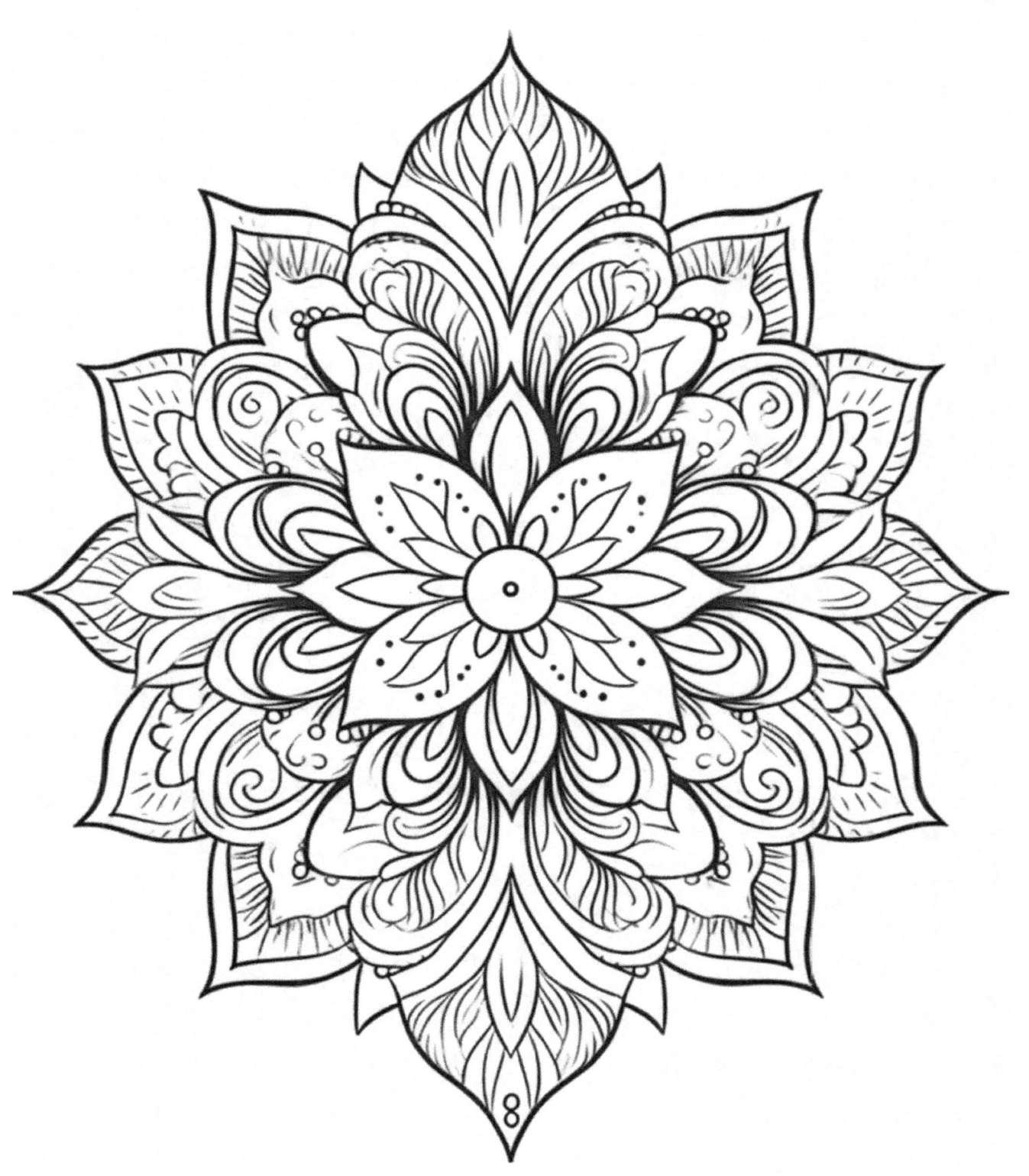

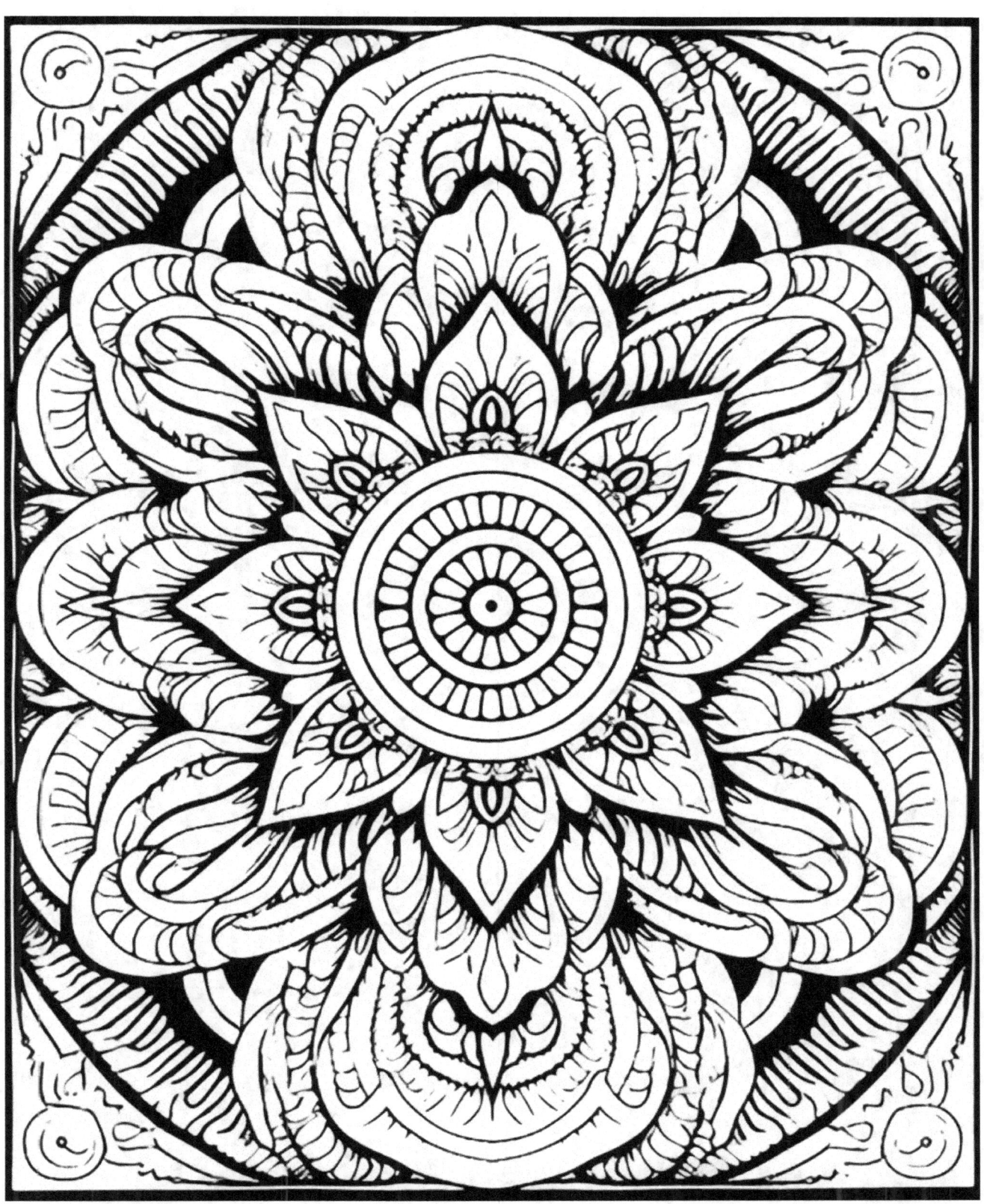

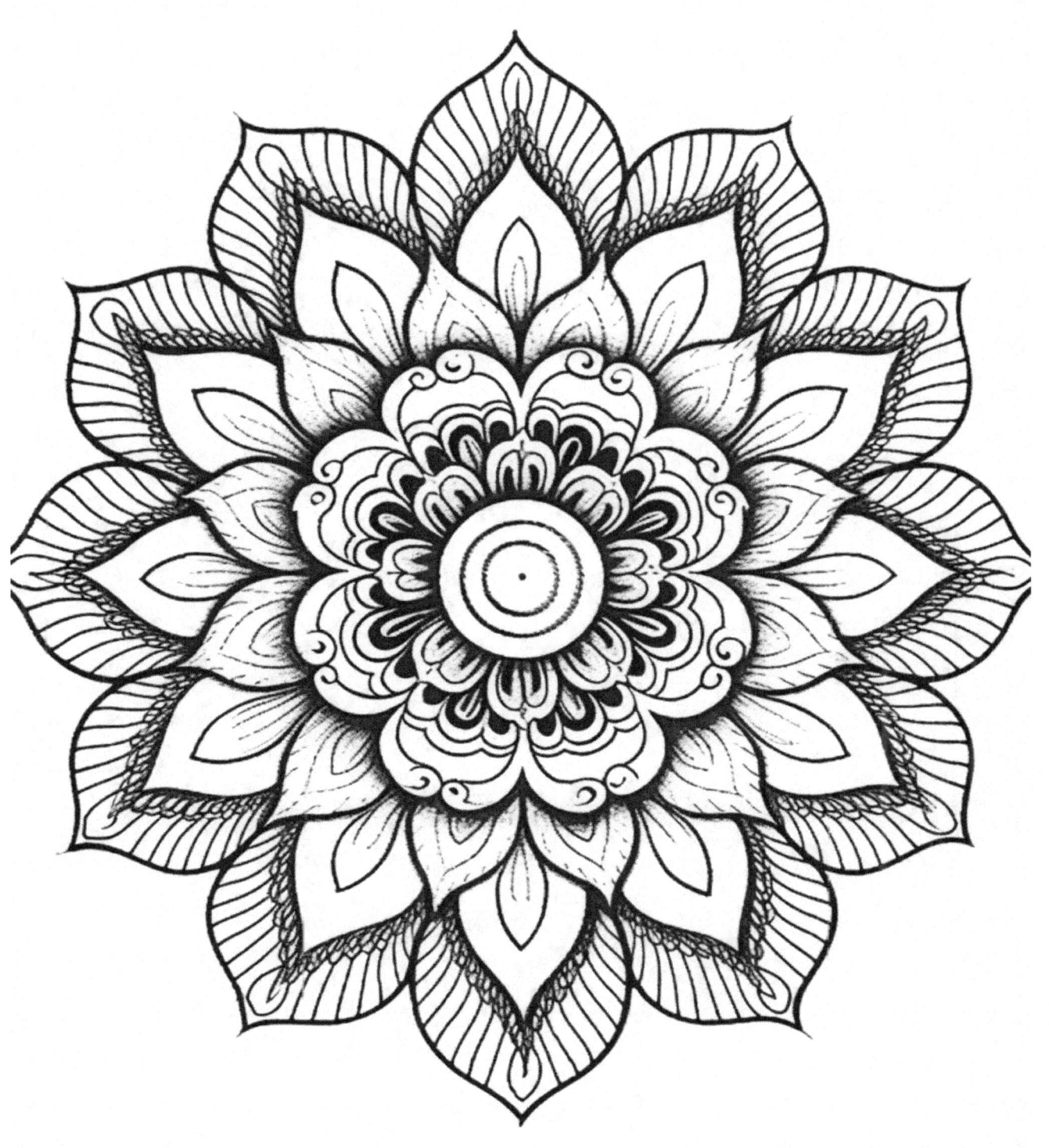

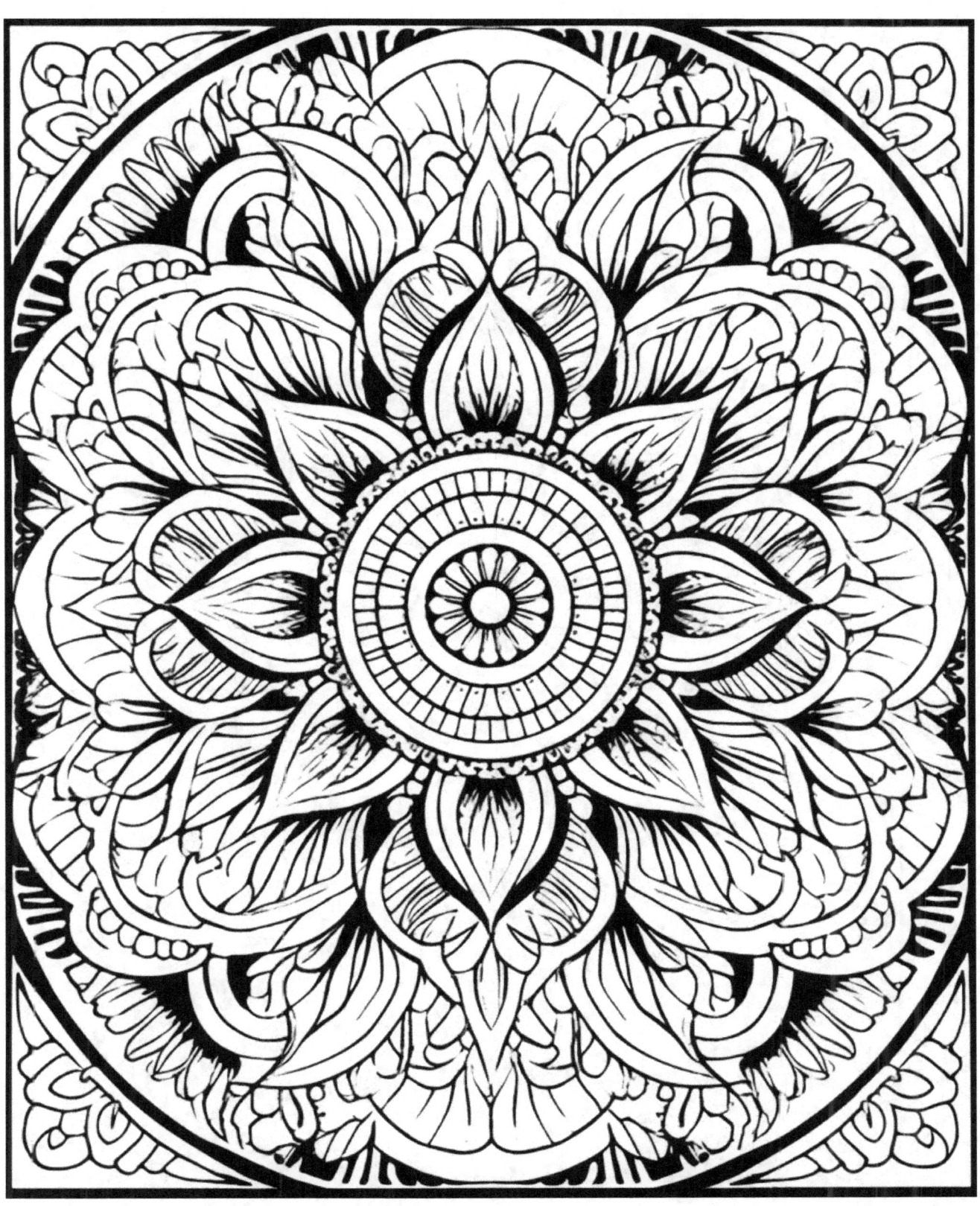

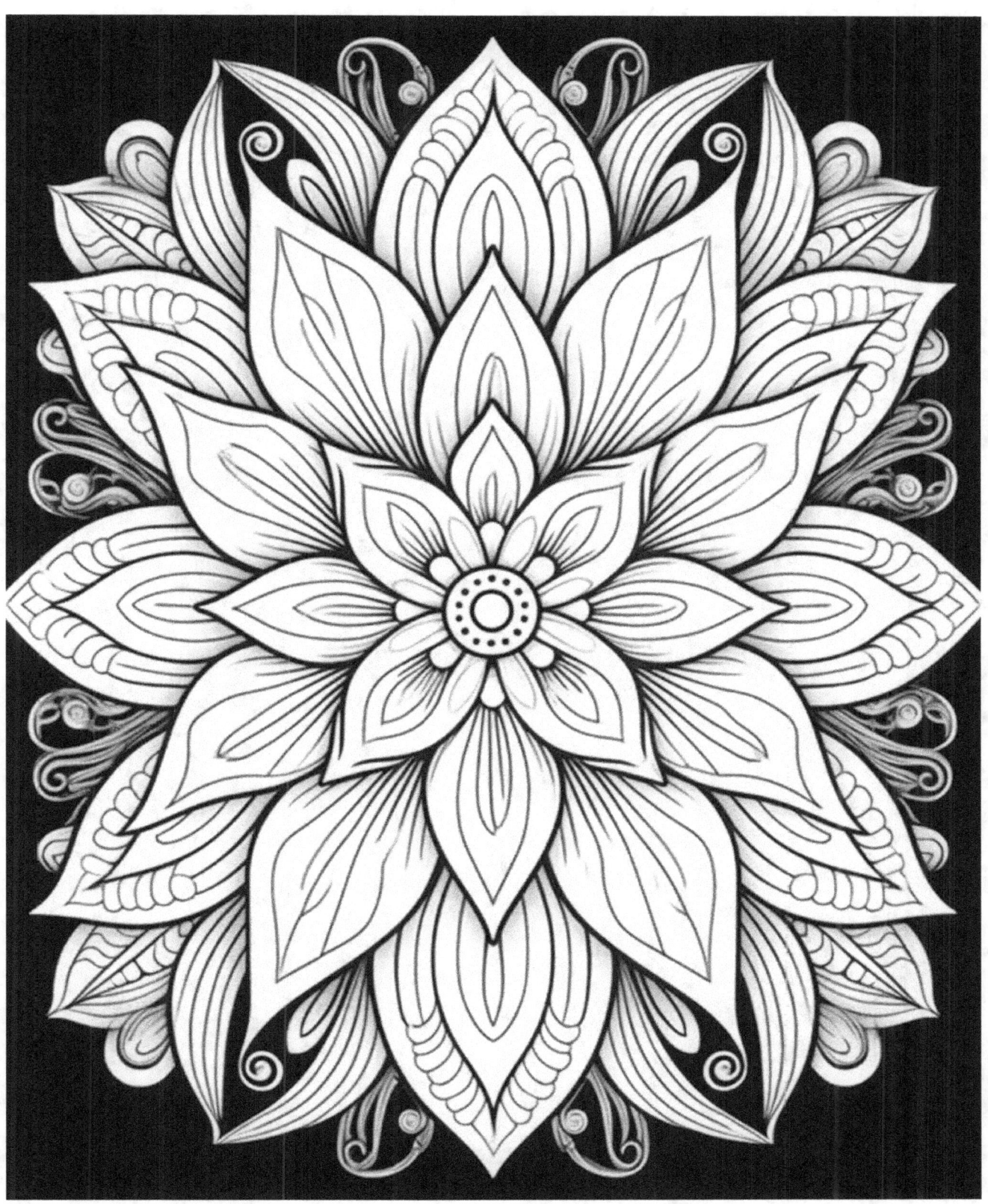

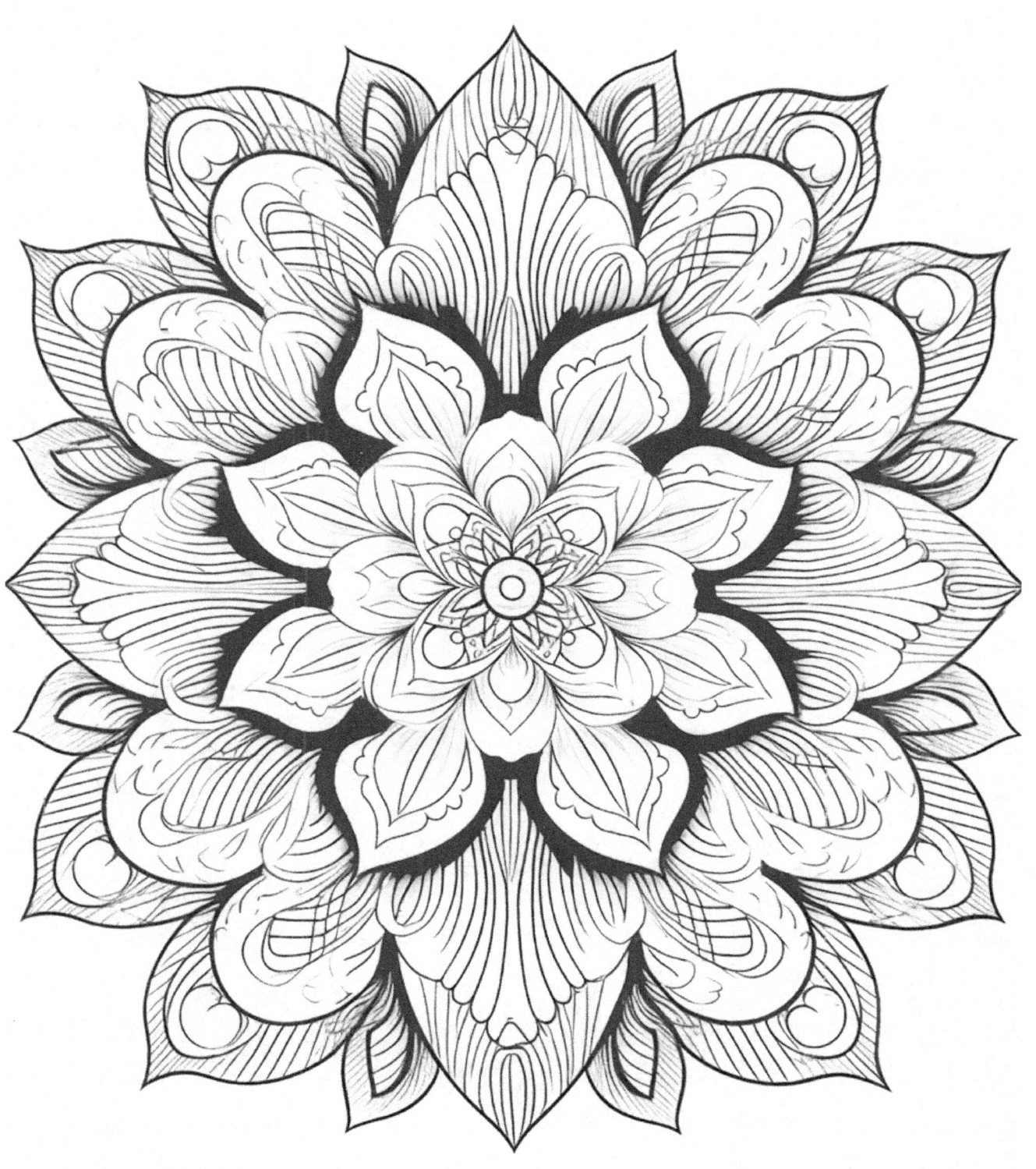

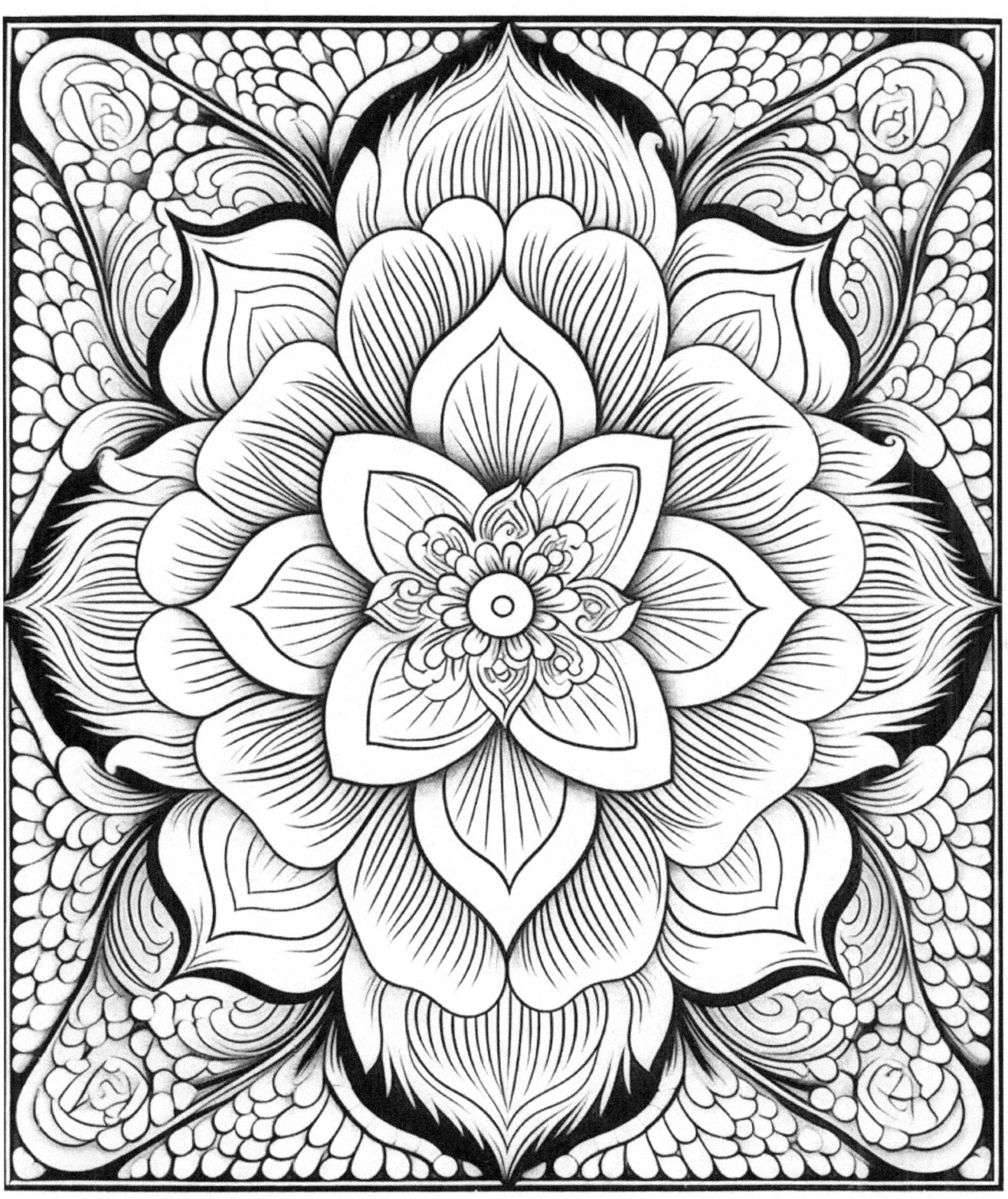

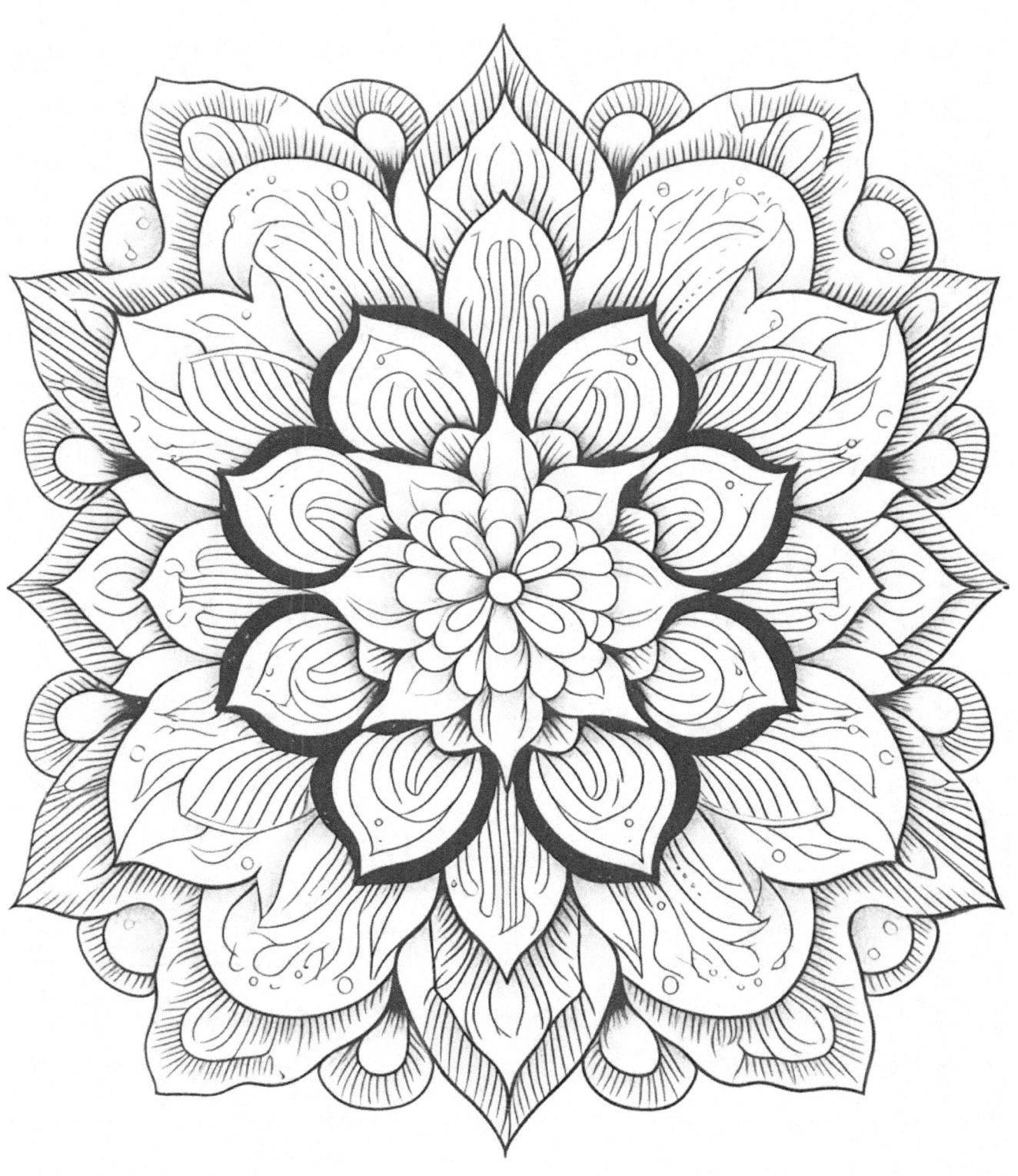

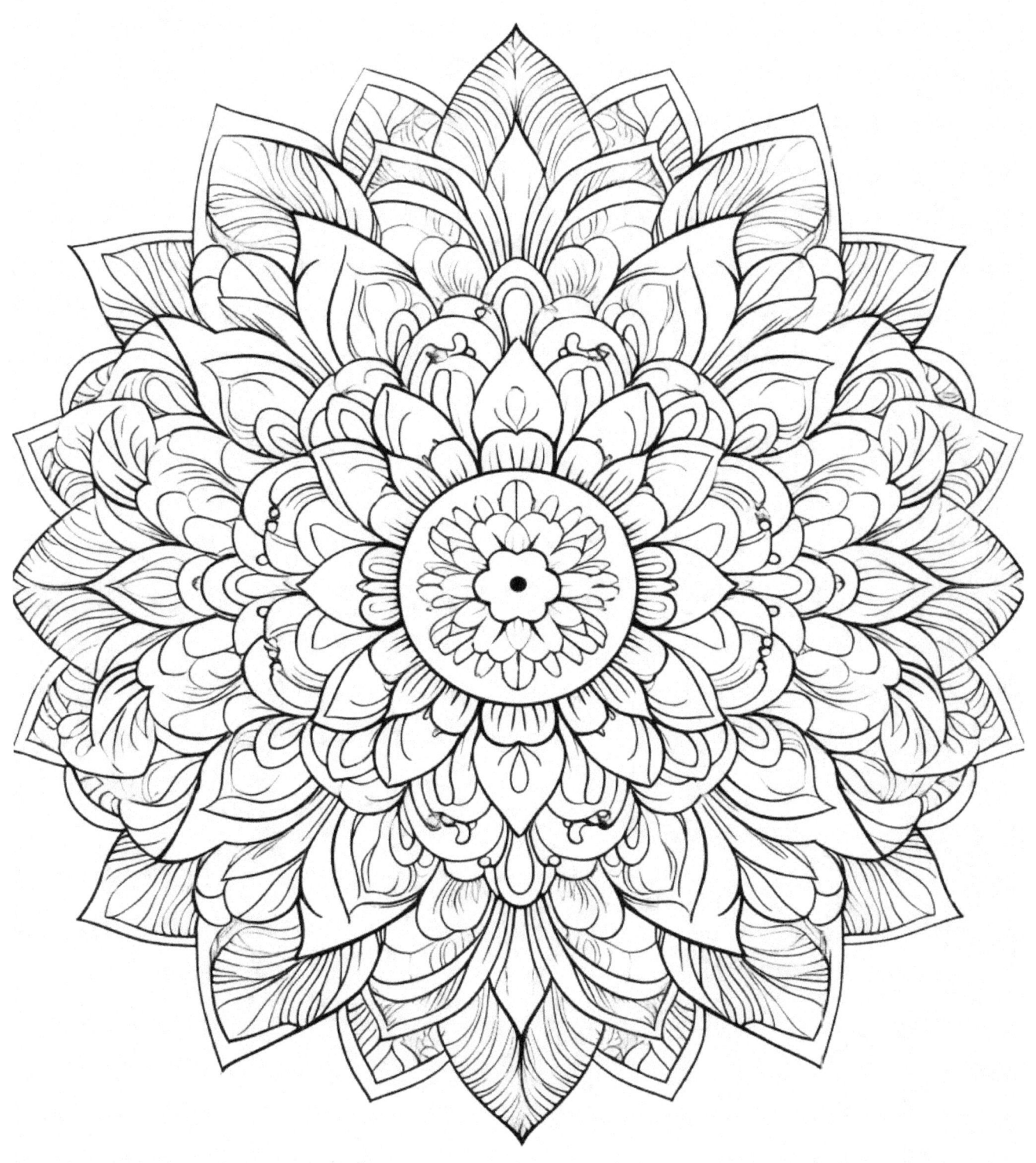

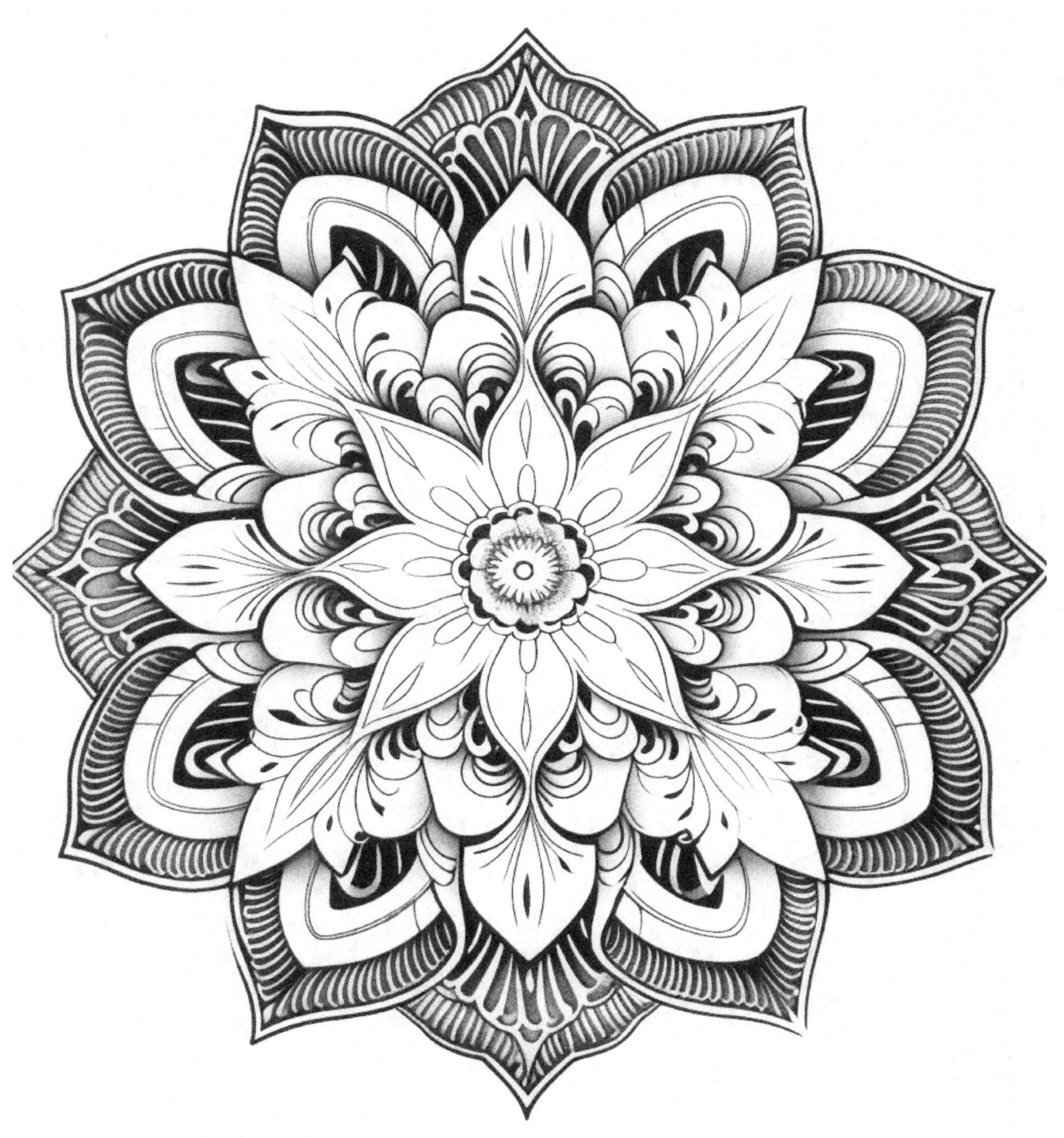

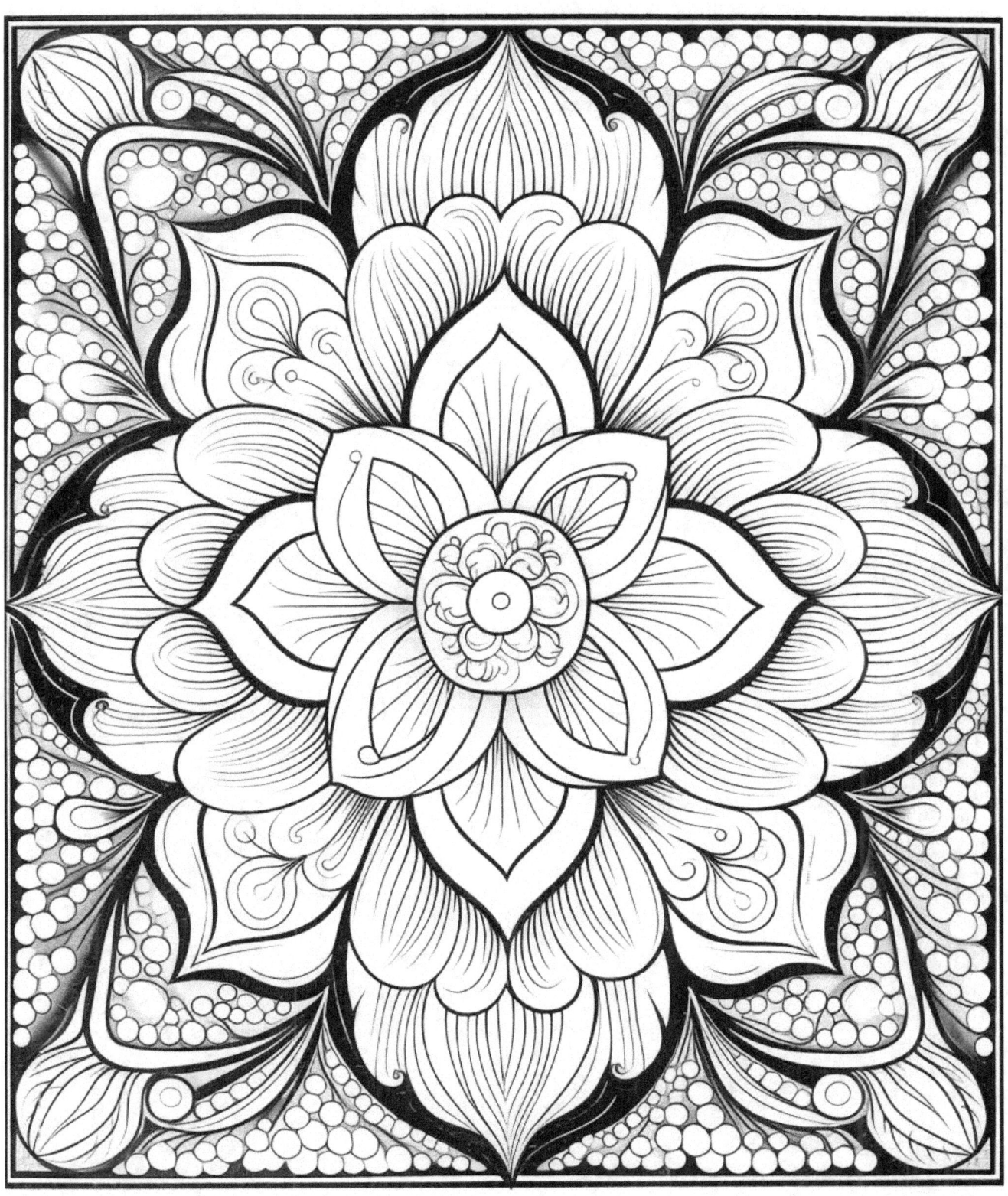

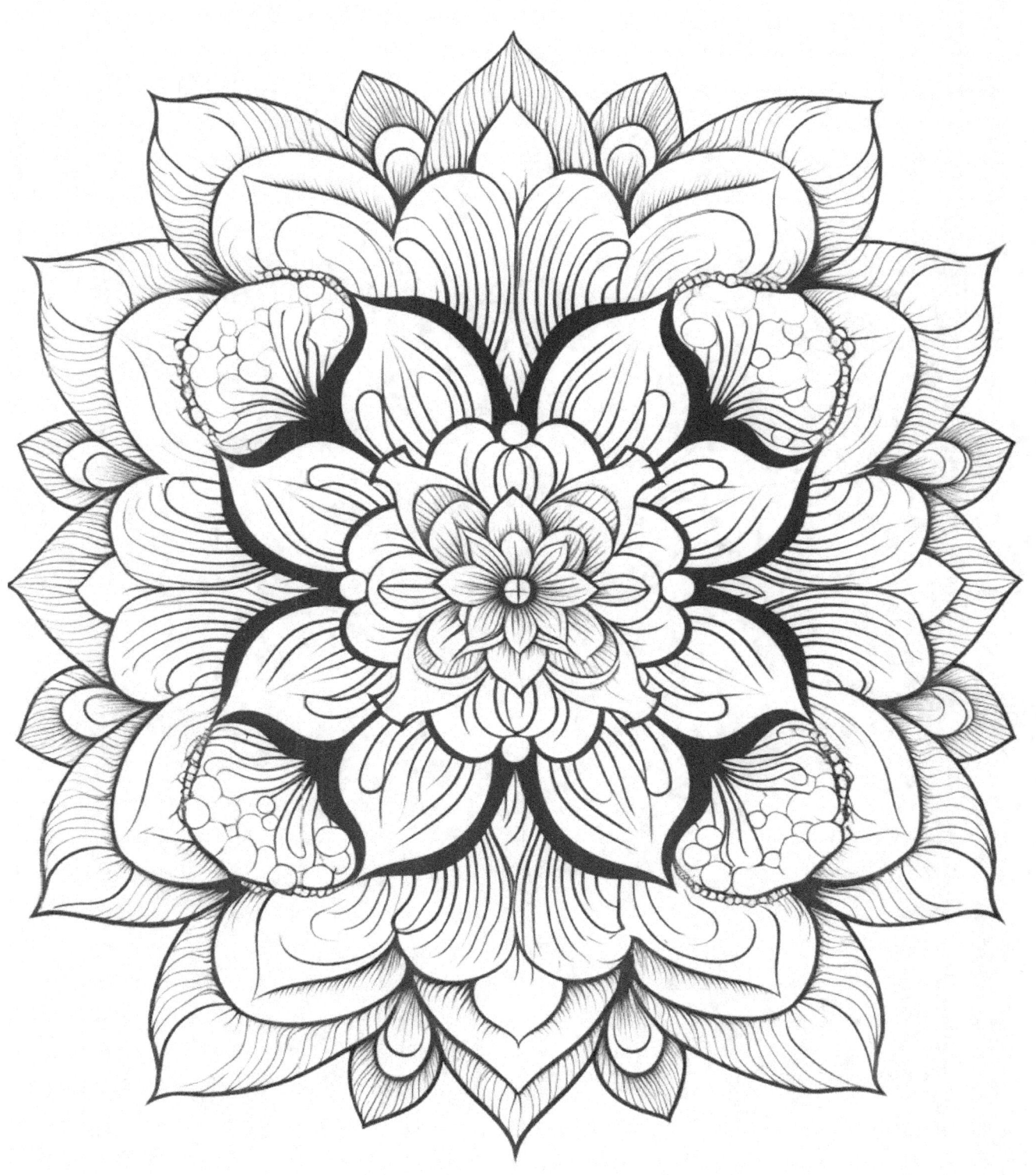

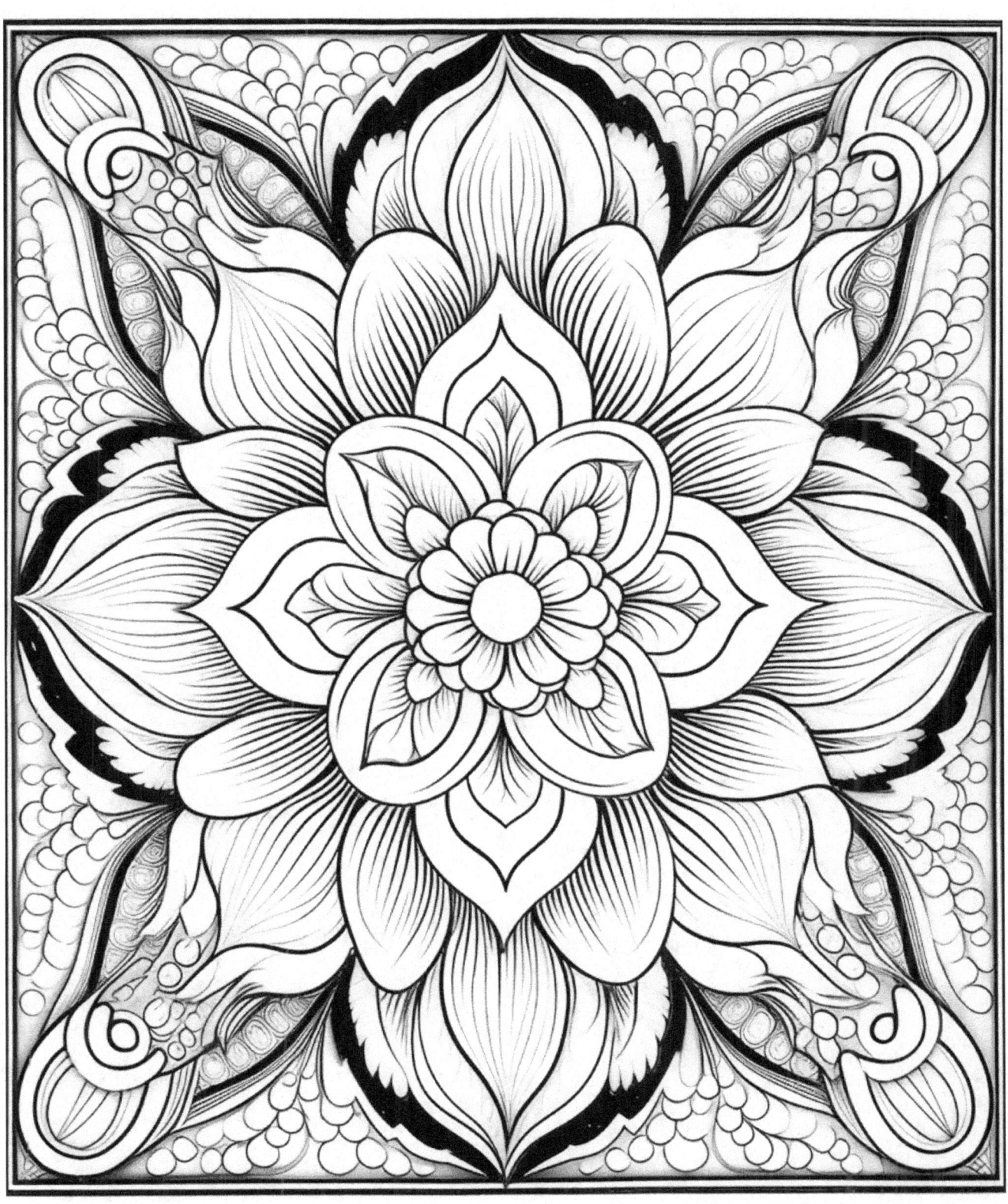